THEOLOGY OF MONEY

Dr. Maxwell Shimba

Shimba Publishing, LLC

Printed in the United States of America

First Printing Edition 2024

TABLE OF CONTENTS

INTRODUCTION

Understanding the plan of God's divine purpose is essential for grasping His overarching intentions. This preface delves into the central mark of God's plan and its profound impact on the lives of believers.

The Vision of God's Plan

From the very beginning, God has intended to work Himself into us, transforming us into His image. This divine goal is realized through the three Persons of the Godhead—the Father, the Son, and the Spirit. As 1 Timothy 1:4 states, "God's plan, which is in faith," highlighting the necessity of understanding and participating in this divine plan.

The Meaning of the Plan

The Greek word for plan, "oikonomia," encompasses administration, stewardship, government, arrangement, and dispensation. In the context of God's purpose, it signifies the dispensing of God Himself into humanity. This concept is fundamental to God's creation and redemption. God's aim is to infuse His essence into us, transforming us into vessels of His divine life.

The Triune God's Plan

God's plan unfolds through the Father is embodied in the Son and the Son being realized in the Spirit. This divine process goes beyond teaching the doctrine of the Trinity; it involves experiencing the practical reality of God's dispensing work. The Scriptures reveal this plan through the incarnation, crucifixion, resurrection, and ascension of Christ.

The Four Major Steps

1. Incarnation: The Father embodied Himself in the Son, bringing the divine nature into humanity. As John 1:14 proclaims, "And the Word became flesh and dwelt among us."

2. Crucifixion: On the cross, all negative things, including sin and death, were dealt with and terminated. Colossians 2:14-15 declares, "He canceled the record of the charges against us and took it away by nailing it to the cross."

3. Resurrection: Christ's resurrection uplifted humanity and brought human nature into God. 1 Corinthians 15:20 affirms, "But Christ has been raised from the dead, the first fruits of those who have fallen asleep."

4. Ascension: Christ's ascension and enthronement as the glorified God-man signify the ultimate victory and the commencement of the Church's mission. Ephesians 1:20-23 describes Christ's exaltation and authority over all things.

The Dispensation of God

God's plan involves the continuous dispensing of His life into us, transforming us into His image. This process requires our cooperation and active participation. As believers, we must engage in practices that facilitate God's work within us, such as prayer, meditation on Scripture, and fellowship with other believers.

The Ultimate Consummation

The ultimate aim of God's plan is the mingling of God with man, culminating in the New Jerusalem. Revelation 21:3-4 envisions this reality: "Behold, the dwelling place of God is with man. He will dwell with them, and they will be his people, and God himself will be with them as their God." The New Jerusalem symbolizes the final and complete union of God and His people, where His glory is fully manifested.

Conclusion

The vision of the mark of God's plan is central to understanding His divine purpose. By recognizing and participating in this divine dispensing, we align ourselves with God's ultimate intention. This vision transforms our lives, enabling us to become the living testimony of God's presence and glory in the world.

DR. MAXWELL SHIMBA

CHAPTER 1

THE ORIGINS OF CURRENCY

The concept of money is deeply rooted in the history of human civilization. From the earliest barter systems to the sophisticated monetary systems of today, currency has played a pivotal role in shaping societies and economies. This chapter delves into the origins of currency, tracing its development through various cultures and examining its role in early societies.

The Barter System

Before the advent of money, ancient civilizations relied on barter as a means of exchange. In this system, goods and services were traded directly for other goods and services. For instance, a farmer might exchange grain for a pot crafted by a potter. While barter allowed for the exchange of goods, it was limited by the need for a double coincidence of wants;

both parties had to have something the other wanted. This limitation is reminiscent of Ecclesiastes 10:19, "A feast is made for laughter, wine makes life merry, and money is the answer for everything," highlighting the necessity of a more efficient means of trade.

The Emergence of Commodity Money

To overcome the limitations of barter, many cultures began using commodity money—items with intrinsic value that were widely accepted in trade. Examples include cattle, grain, shells, and metals. These commodities served as a medium of exchange, a unit of account, and a store of value, thus laying the foundation for more sophisticated monetary systems. Proverbs 11:1 teaches, "The Lord detests dishonest scales, but accurate weights find favor with him," underscoring the importance of fairness and standardization in trade.

Metallurgy and the Birth of Coinage

The development of metallurgy around 3000 BCE marked a significant milestone in the history of money. Societies discovered that metals like gold, silver, and copper could be molded into standardized units of value. These early coins were stamped with symbols to denote their weight and authenticity, facilitating trade and reducing the need for complex bartering. Job 28:1-2 mentions, "There is a mine for silver and a place where gold is refined. Iron is taken from the earth, and copper is smelted from ore," reflecting the early use of metals in trade.

Money in Ancient Civilizations

Several ancient civilizations made significant contributions to the development of currency:

1. Mesopotamia: The Sumerians in Mesopotamia were among the first to use standardized weights of silver as a form of money. The concept of using a specific weight of metal as currency was revolutionary and laid the groundwork for future monetary systems.

2. Egypt: The ancient Egyptians used rings made of precious metals as currency. These rings, known as "shat," were used in trade and to pay workers, including those who built the pyramids. This practice aligns with Genesis 23:16,

where Abraham weighed out silver to buy a field, demonstrating the use of precious metals in transactions.

3. China: The Chinese initially used cowrie shells as money. By 1000 BCE, they transitioned to metal currency, casting bronze replicas of cowrie shells and later evolving into round coins with square holes, which became the standard form of Chinese currency for centuries.

4. Greece and Rome: The Greeks and Romans further advanced the use of coins. Greek city-states minted their coins, often featuring images of gods and heroes. The Roman Empire standardized currency across its vast territories, using coins made of gold, silver, and bronze to facilitate trade and taxation. Matthew 22:19-21 reflects this with Jesus' reference to the denarius, a Roman coin when discussing taxes.

The Role of Money in Early Societies

In early societies, money served several crucial functions:

1. Medium of Exchange: Money simplified trade by eliminating the need for a double coincidence of wants. It

provided a common denominator for valuing goods and services, making transactions more efficient. Proverbs 16:16 states, "How much better to get wisdom than gold, to get insight rather than silver!" highlighting the value of efficient trade.

2. Unit of Account: Money provided a standard measure of value, allowing individuals and businesses to price goods and services consistently. This standardization was essential for record-keeping and economic planning.

3. Store of Value: Money allows individuals to save and accumulate wealth. Unlike perishable goods, money could be stored and used in the future, enabling long-term planning and investment. Matthew 6:19-21 advises, "Do not store up for yourselves treasures on earth, where moths and vermin destroy, and where thieves break in and steal. But store up for yourselves treasures in heaven," yet acknowledges the practical use of storing wealth.

4. Facilitator of Social and Economic Structures: Money played a key role in the development of social hierarchies and economic systems. It enabled the collection of taxes, the payment of wages, and the accumulation of

wealth, which in turn influenced social and political dynamics. This is seen in Ecclesiastes 5:10, "Whoever loves money never has enough; whoever loves wealth is never satisfied with their income," highlighting the complexities of wealth accumulation.

Conclusion

The origins of currency reflect humanity's ingenuity in overcoming the limitations of barter and developing systems that facilitate trade and economic growth. From commodity money to the standardized coins of ancient civilizations, the evolution of currency has been instrumental in shaping societies and their economic structures. As we move forward in this book, we will explore how these early developments laid the foundation for modern monetary systems and continue to influence contemporary theological and ethical discussions about money.

CHAPTER 2

THE THEOLOGY OF MONEY IN THE BOOK OF GENESIS

The book of Genesis, as the first book of the Bible, lays the foundational principles for understanding God's creation, human stewardship, and the appropriate attitudes towards resources, including money. While the explicit concept of money as we understand it today does not appear in Genesis, the principles of stewardship, generosity, and responsibility are woven throughout the narrative. This chapter explores the theology of money in Genesis, examining God's plan for resource management and the attitudes expected of humanity during and after creation.

God's Creation and Human Stewardship

1. Creation Mandate:

- Genesis 1:26-28: "Then God said, 'Let us make mankind in our image, in our likeness, so that they may rule over the fish in the sea and the birds in the sky, over the livestock and all the wild animals, and over all the creatures that move along the ground.' So God created mankind in his own image, in the image of God he created them; male and female he created them. God blessed them and said to them, 'Be fruitful and increase in number; fill the earth and subdue it. Rule over the fish in the sea and the birds in the sky and over every living creature that moves on the ground.'"

The creation mandate highlights human beings' responsibility to manage and care for the Earth. This dominion involves stewardship of resources, implying a balanced and respectful use of what God has provided. The mandate sets the tone for attitudes towards resources, emphasizing responsible management rather than exploitation.

"And God said, Let us make man in our image, after our likeness: and let them have dominion over the fish of the sea, and over the fowl of the air, and over the cattle, and over all the earth, and over every creeping thing that creepeth upon the earth." (Genesis 1:26, KJV)

Interpretation:

In this verse, God declares His intention to create humankind in His image and likeness. This denotes a special status for humans among creation, reflecting God's nature in some capacity. Additionally, God grants humans dominion over all other living creatures on earth, indicating a stewardship role.

Commentary:

"And God said": This phrase emphasizes the creative power and authority of God. The divine speech act initiates the creation of humankind, demonstrating God's intentional and purposeful action in creation (Psalm 33:9).

"Let us make man in our image, after our likeness": The plural language ("us" and "our") has been the subject of much theological discussion. It could be understood as a reflection of the divine council or the Trinity. "Image" and "likeness" suggest that humans reflect certain aspects of God's nature, such as rationality, moral capacity, relationality, and authority (Genesis 9:6; James 3:9).

"And let them have dominion over the fish of the sea, and over the fowl of the air, and over the cattle, and over all the earth, and over every creeping thing that creepeth upon the earth": God grants humans dominion over other creatures, indicating a responsibility to govern and steward creation wisely and benevolently. This dominion is not about exploitation but about stewardship and care (Psalm 8:6-8).

Concordance:

- And God said: This phrase is repeated throughout Genesis 1, emphasizing the power of God's word in creation (Psalm 33:9).

- Let us make man in our image, after our likeness: This statement highlights the unique creation of humans in the image of God, reflecting His nature and attributes (Genesis 9:6; James 3:9).

- And let them have dominion: This phrase grants humans authority over creation, indicating a stewardship role that requires responsible and ethical management of the environment and its creatures (Psalm 8:6-8).

References from the King James Bible:

1. Psalm 33:9: "For he spake, and it was done; he commanded, and it stood fast."

2. Genesis 9:6: "Whoso sheddeth man's blood, by man shall his blood be shed: for in the image of God made he man."

3. James 3:9: "Therewith bless we God, even the Father; and therewith curse we men, which are made after the similitude of God."

4. Psalm 8:6-8: "Thou madest him to have dominion over the works of thy hands; thou hast put all things under his feet: All sheep and oxen, yea, and the beasts of the field; The fowl of the air, and the fish of the sea, and whatsoever passeth through the paths of the seas."

Interpretation and Application:

- Imago Dei (Image of God): Being made in the image of God imparts inherent dignity and worth to every human being. This concept is foundational to Christian ethics and the understanding of human nature.

- Plurality in Creation: The use of plural pronouns in "Let us make man" suggests a communal aspect to God's nature, which Christians often interpret as the Trinity. This highlights the relational aspect of God and humanity.

- Dominion and Stewardship: Human dominion over creation implies responsibility and care. Christians are called to steward the environment and all living creatures wisely, reflecting God's care and order in creation.

"So God created man in his own image, in the image of God created he him; male and female created he them." (Genesis 1:27, KJV)

Interpretation:

This verse emphasizes the creation of humankind by God, highlighting that humans are made in the image of God. It also stresses the creation of both male and female, indicating equality and complementarity in the human species.

Commentary:

"So God created man in his own image": This phrase reiterates the unique status of humans in creation. Being created in God's image means that humans reflect certain attributes of God, such as rationality, morality, creativity, and the ability to relate to others (Genesis 9:6; Colossians 3:10).

"In the image of God created he him": The repetition underscores the importance of this concept. It reinforces that the image of God is intrinsic to all humans, providing a foundation for human dignity and worth (James 3:9).

"Male and female created he them": This part of the verse highlights the creation of both genders, affirming that both male and female are made in God's image. This establishes the equality of the sexes and the idea that both are necessary for the fullness of humanity (Galatians 3:28).

Concordance:

- So God created man in his own image: This phrase emphasizes the unique creation of humans as bearers of God's image, highlighting their special status in creation (Genesis 5:1-2; Colossians 3:10).
- In the image of God created he him: The repetition underscores the significance of being made in God's image, affirming the inherent dignity and worth of every person (James 3:9).
- Male and female created he them: This statement highlights the creation of both genders in God's image,

emphasizing equality and complementarity between men and women (Galatians 3:28).

References from the King James Bible:

1. Genesis 9:6: "Whoso sheddeth man's blood, by man shall his blood be shed: for in the image of God made he man."

2. Colossians 3:10: "And have put on the new man, which is renewed in knowledge after the image of him that created him:"

3. James 3:9: "Therewith bless we God, even the Father; and therewith curse we men, which are made after the similitude of God."

4. Genesis 5:1-2: "This is the book of the generations of Adam. In the day that God created man, in the likeness of God made he him; Male and female created he them; and blessed them, and called their name Adam, in the day when they were created."

5. Galatians 3:28: "There is neither Jew nor Greek, there is neither bond nor free, there is neither male nor female: for ye are all one in Christ Jesus."

Interpretation and Application:

- Imago Dei (Image of God): This concept is foundational to understanding human nature, dignity, and worth. Every person, regardless of gender, reflects God's image and therefore possesses inherent value.

- Equality and Complementarity: The creation of male and female in God's image emphasizes the equality of the sexes and their complementary roles. Both are essential to the full expression of humanity and the image of God.

- Human Dignity: The image of God in humans forms the basis for the sanctity of life and ethical behavior. It calls for respect, justice, and love towards all people, recognizing their worth as God's image-bearers.

"And God blessed them, and God said unto them, Be fruitful, and multiply, and replenish the earth, and subdue it: and have dominion over the fish of the sea, and over the fowl of the air, and over every living thing that moveth upon the earth." (Genesis 1:28, KJV)

Interpretation:

In this verse, God blesses the first humans, commanding them to be fruitful and multiply, to fill the earth and subdue it, and to exercise dominion over all living creatures. This passage outlines the role and responsibility of humanity in creation.

Commentary:

"And God blessed them": God's blessing indicates His favor and endowment of the ability to fulfill His commands. Blessing in this context involves the empowerment to be fruitful and to exercise dominion (Genesis 9:1).

"And God said unto them, Be fruitful, and multiply, and replenish the earth": This command to be fruitful and multiply establishes the importance of procreation and the spreading of humanity across the earth. "Replenish" suggests filling the earth, indicating a need to populate and steward the land (Genesis 9:7).

"And subdue it": The term "subdue" indicates bringing the earth under control and harnessing its potential. This implies not exploitation but responsible stewardship, managing the resources of the earth wisely (Psalm 8:6-8).

"And have dominion over the fish of the sea, and over the fowl of the air, and over every living thing that moveth upon the earth": Dominion here refers to authority and stewardship over creation. Humans are entrusted with the responsibility to care for and manage the animal kingdom and the environment, reflecting God's rule (Genesis 1:26; Psalm 115:16).

Concordance:

- And God blessed them: This phrase signifies God's favor and empowerment to fulfill His commands, marking the beginning of human purpose and responsibility (Genesis 9:1).

- Be fruitful, and multiply, and replenish the earth: This command emphasizes procreation and the spread of humanity, indicating the role of humans in filling and managing the earth (Genesis 9:7).

- And subdue it: This term suggests bringing the earth under control and managing its resources responsibly, highlighting the role of stewardship (Psalm 8:6-8).

- And have dominion: This phrase indicates the authority and responsibility given to humans to care for and manage creation, reflecting God's rule (Genesis 1:26; Psalm 115:16).

References from the King James Bible:

1. Genesis 9:1: "And God blessed Noah and his sons, and said unto them, Be fruitful, and multiply, and replenish the earth."

2. Genesis 9:7: "And you, be ye fruitful, and multiply; bring forth abundantly in the earth, and multiply therein."

3. Psalm 8:6-8: "Thou madest him to have dominion over the works of thy hands; thou hast put all things under his feet: All sheep and oxen, yea, and the beasts of the field; The fowl of the air, and the fish of the sea, and whatsoever passeth through the paths of the seas."

4. Genesis 1:26: "And God said, Let us make man in our image, after our likeness: and let them have dominion over the fish of the sea, and over the fowl of the air, and over the cattle, and over all the earth, and over every creeping thing that creepeth upon the earth."

5. Psalm 115:16: "The heaven, even the heavens, are the Lord's: but the earth hath he given to the children of men."

Interpretation and Application:

- Blessing and Purpose: God's blessing underscores the purpose and mission given to humanity. Humans are to be fruitful, multiply, and responsibly manage the earth, reflecting God's care and creativity.

- Stewardship and Responsibility: The command to subdue and have dominion over the earth highlights the responsibility of humans to care for creation wisely and ethically. This stewardship role calls for sustainable practices that honor God's creation.

- Human Authority: Dominion over the animal kingdom and the environment indicates a hierarchical structure in creation. However, this authority is meant to reflect God's righteous and benevolent rule, not exploitation or abuse.

2. Provision and Abundance:

- Genesis 2:15-16: "The Lord God took the man and put him in the Garden of Eden to work it and take care of it. And the Lord God commanded the man, 'You are free to eat from any tree in the garden.'"

Interpretation:

In these verses, God places Adam in the Garden of Eden with the responsibility to cultivate and maintain it. God also grants Adam the freedom to eat from every tree in the garden, signifying provision and abundance. This highlights both the stewardship role given to humanity and God's generous provision for their needs.

Commentary:

Verse 15:

"And the Lord God took the man, and put him into the garden of Eden to dress it and to keep it": God places Adam in the Garden of Eden, assigning him the roles of caretaker and steward. "To dress it" means to cultivate and tend the garden, while "to keep it" implies protecting and preserving it. This reflects humanity's responsibility to manage and steward creation responsibly (Genesis 2:8; Genesis 3:23).

Verse 16:

"And the Lord God commanded the man, saying, Of every tree of the garden thou mayest freely eat": God generously provides for Adam, allowing him to eat freely from every tree in the garden except one (as stated in the following verse). This indicates God's abundant provision and the freedom given to humanity within the boundaries set by God (Genesis 1:29; Genesis 2:9).

Concordance:

Verse 15:

- And the Lord God took the man: This phrase shows God's direct involvement in placing Adam in the garden, emphasizing His care and intentionality (Genesis 2:8).

- To dress it and to keep it: These terms indicate the roles of cultivation and stewardship assigned to Adam, highlighting the responsibility given to humanity to manage and care for creation (Genesis 3:23).

Verse 16:

- And the Lord God commanded the man: This phrase introduces God's command, showing His authority and the instruction given to humanity (Genesis 1:28).

- Of every tree of the garden thou mayest freely eat: This statement highlights God's generous provision and the abundance available to humanity within the garden (Genesis 1:29; Genesis 2:9).

References from the King James Bible:

1. Genesis 2:8: "And the Lord God planted a garden eastward in Eden; and there he put the man whom he had formed."

2. Genesis 3:23: "Therefore the Lord God sent him forth from the garden of Eden, to till the ground from whence he was taken."

3. Genesis 1:29: "And God said, Behold, I have given you every herb bearing seed, which is upon the face of all the earth, and every tree, in the which is the fruit of a tree yielding seed; to you it shall be for meat."

4. Genesis 2:9: "And out of the ground made the Lord God to grow every tree that is pleasant to the sight, and good for food; the tree of life also in the midst of the garden, and the tree of knowledge of good and evil."

5. Genesis 1:28: "And God blessed them, and God said unto them, Be fruitful, and multiply, and replenish the earth, and subdue it: and have dominion over the fish of the sea, and over the fowl of the air, and over every living thing that moveth upon the earth."

- Provision: God's placement of Adam in the Garden of Eden and the command to eat freely from every tree (except one) highlight the provision made for humanity. God provides not just the necessities but an abundance of resources for Adam's sustenance and enjoyment.

- Abundance: The phrase "thou mayest freely eat" underscores the generosity of God's provision. The garden is filled with a variety of trees that are both pleasant to the sight and good for food, indicating the richness and diversity of God's creation intended for humanity's benefit.

Application:

- Stewardship: Humanity's role as stewards of creation is a significant theme. God entrusts humans with the responsibility to cultivate and care for the environment, reflecting His own care and creativity.

- Gratitude and Responsibility: The abundant provision should inspire gratitude in humans and a recognition of the responsibility that comes with managing God's gifts wisely and ethically.

- Boundaries and Freedom: While God provides abundantly, He also sets boundaries (as seen in the subsequent verses). Respecting these boundaries is essential for maintaining a right relationship with God and His creation.

The Fall and Its Impact on Resource Management

1. The Disobedience of Adam and Eve:

- Genesis 3:17-19: "To Adam, he said, 'Because you listened to your wife and ate fruit from the tree about which I commanded you, "You must not eat from it," cursed is the ground because of you; through painful toil, you will eat food from it all the days of your life. It will produce thorns and thistles for you, and you will eat the plants of the field. By the sweat of your brow, you will eat your food until you return to the ground since from it you were taken; for dust you are and to dust you will return.'"

Interpretation:

In these verses, God pronounces the consequences of Adam's disobedience. The ground is cursed because of Adam, making his work laborious and full of hardship. The passage also highlights the inevitability of death, emphasizing human mortality and the return to dust from which humans were formed.

Commentary:

Verse 17:

"And unto Adam he said, Because thou hast hearkened unto the voice of thy wife, and hast eaten of the tree, of which I commanded thee, saying, Thou shalt not eat of it: cursed is the ground for thy sake; in sorrow shalt thou eat of it all the days of thy life;"

- "Because thou hast hearkened unto the voice of thy wife": Adam is held accountable for his disobedience, particularly because he listened to his wife over God's command (Genesis 2:16-17).

- "And hast eaten of the tree, of which I commanded thee, saying, Thou shalt not eat of it": This specifies Adam's direct disobedience to God's clear command.

- "Cursed is the ground for thy sake": The ground itself is cursed as a result of Adam's sin, indicating that sin affects not just the sinner but all of creation (Romans 8:20-22).

- "In sorrow shalt thou eat of it all the days of thy life": Adam's work, which was initially a joyful stewardship, becomes toilsome and filled with sorrow and hardship.

Verse 18:

"Thorns also and thistles shall it bring forth to thee; and thou shalt eat the herb of the field;"

- "Thorns also and thistles shall it bring forth to thee": The ground will produce weeds and obstacles, symbolizing the increased difficulty in labor and the presence of futility in human efforts (Hebrews 6:8).
- "Thou shalt eat the herb of the field": This indicates a change in humanity's diet to include the harder-to-obtain vegetation, contrasting with the ease of eating from the garden's trees (Genesis 1:29).

Verse 19:

"In the sweat of thy face shalt thou eat bread, till thou return unto the ground; for out of it wast thou taken: for dust thou art, and unto dust shalt thou return."

- "In the sweat of thy face shalt thou eat bread": Adam will now have to labor intensively to produce food, signifying the struggle for survival (Ecclesiastes 2:22-23).
- "Till thou return unto the ground": This points to the inevitability of death as a result of sin, fulfilling God's warning that disobedience would lead to death (Genesis 2:17).

- "For out of it wast thou taken: for dust thou art, and unto dust shalt thou return": This reinforces the mortality of humans, reminding Adam (and all humanity) of their origins from the earth and their eventual return to it (Psalm 90:3).

Concordance:

- Because thou hast hearkened unto the voice of thy wife: This highlights the consequence of prioritizing human counsel over God's command (Genesis 2:16-17).
- Cursed is the ground for thy sake: Sin affects all creation, not just the sinner (Romans 8:20-22).
- Thorns also and thistles shall it bring forth to thee: Represents the increased difficulty and futility in human labor (Hebrews 6:8).
- In the sweat of thy face shalt thou eat bread: Signifies the struggle and hard work now required to obtain food (Ecclesiastes 2:22-23).
- For dust thou art, and unto dust shalt thou return: Emphasizes human mortality and the return to the earth (Psalm 90:3).

References from the King James Bible:

1. Genesis 2:16-17: "And the Lord God commanded the man, saying, Of every tree of the garden thou mayest freely eat: But of the tree of the knowledge of good and evil, thou shalt not eat of it: for in the day that thou eatest thereof thou shalt surely die."

2. Romans 8:20-22: "For the creature was made subject to vanity, not willingly, but by reason of him who hath subjected the same in hope, Because the creature itself also shall be delivered from the bondage of corruption into the glorious liberty of the children of God. For we know that the whole creation groaneth and travaileth in pain together until now."

3. Hebrews 6:8: "But that which beareth thorns and briers is rejected, and is nigh unto cursing; whose end is to be burned."

4. Genesis 1:29: "And God said, Behold, I have given you every herb bearing seed, which is upon the face of all the earth, and every tree, in the which is the fruit of a tree yielding seed; to you it shall be for meat."

5. Ecclesiastes 2:22-23: "For what hath man of all his labour, and of the vexation of his heart, wherein he hath laboured under the sun? For all his days are sorrows, and his travail grief; yea, his heart taketh not rest in the night. This is also vanity."

6. Psalm 90:3: "Thou turnest man to destruction; and sayest, Return, ye children of men."

Provision and Abundance:

- Provision: Despite the curse, God still provides for humanity. Adam will eat "the herb of the field" and "bread," indicating that while labor has become toilsome, God has not abandoned His provision for human needs.
- Abundance: The mention of eating bread signifies that there will be enough food to sustain life, even if obtaining it is now fraught with difficulty. God's creation still offers what is necessary for survival, though it now requires hard work to access it.

Application:

- Human Responsibility and Stewardship: These verses remind believers of the serious consequences of disobedience and the importance of faithful stewardship of God's creation, even in a fallen world.
- Understanding Mortality: Acknowledging human mortality ("dust thou art, and unto dust shalt thou return")

encourages a perspective of humility and dependence on God.

- Labor and Provision: The need to labor for sustenance is both a consequence of sin and a continuing opportunity to rely on God's provision and grace.

2. Attitudes Towards Resources Post-Fall:

- Genesis 4:3-5: "In the course of time Cain brought some of the fruits of the soil as an offering to the Lord. And Abel also brought an offering—fat portions from some of the firstborn of his flock. The Lord looked with favor on Abel and his offering, but on Cain and his offering he did not look with favor. So Cain was very angry, and his face was downcast."

Interpretation:

These verses describe the offerings made by Cain and Abel to the Lord. Abel's offering is accepted by God, while Cain's is not. This results in Cain becoming very angry and dejected.

Commentary:

Verse 3:

"And in process of time it came to pass, that Cain brought of the fruit of the ground an offering unto the Lord."

- "In process of time": This phrase indicates the passage of time, suggesting a period during which Cain and Abel grew into adulthood and took on their respective roles.

- "Cain brought of the fruit of the ground an offering unto the Lord": Cain, a farmer, offers some of his produce to God. The nature of the offering—"of the fruit of the ground"—indicates that it was a general offering, not specified as the best or first fruits.

Verse 4:

"And Abel, he also brought of the firstlings of his flock and of the fat thereof. And the Lord had respect unto Abel and to his offering:"

- "Abel, he also brought of the firstlings of his flock and of the fat thereof": Abel, a shepherd, offers the firstborn of his flock and their fat portions. The "firstlings" and "fat" suggest that Abel brought the best of what he had, indicating a sacrificial and devoted heart.

- "And the Lord had respect unto Abel and to his offering": God accepted Abel and his offering, showing favor towards the heart and attitude behind the offering (Hebrews 11:4).

- *"But unto Cain and to his offering he had not respect"*: God did not accept Cain's offering, implying there was something lacking in either the quality of the offering or the attitude behind it (1 John 3:12).

- "And Cain was very wroth, and his countenance fell": Cain's reaction was one of intense anger and dejection, revealing his heart's response to rejection and possibly underlying issues of pride and jealousy.

Concordance:

- Offering: The concept of offerings to God appears throughout the Bible, signifying worship, gratitude, and atonement (Leviticus 1:3; 2:1; Malachi 1:8).

- Respect (regard): God's acceptance or rejection of offerings often relates to the offerer's heart and obedience (Psalm 51:17; Isaiah 1:11-17).

- Wrath and countenance: Anger and dejection are common human responses to rejection and can lead to sin if not addressed (Ephesians 4:26-27; James 1:19-20).

References from the King James Bible:

1. Hebrews 11:4: "By faith Abel offered unto God a more excellent sacrifice than Cain, by which he obtained witness that he was righteous, God testifying of his gifts: and by it he being dead yet speaketh."

2. 1 John 3:12: "Not as Cain, who was of that wicked one, and slew his brother. And wherefore slew he him? Because his own works were evil, and his brother's righteous."

3. Leviticus 1:3: "If his offering be a burnt sacrifice of the herd, let him offer a male without blemish: he shall offer it of his own voluntary will at the door of the tabernacle of the congregation before the Lord."

4. Malachi 1:8: "And if ye offer the blind for sacrifice, is it not evil? and if ye offer the lame and sick, is it not evil? offer it now unto thy governor; will he be pleased with thee, or accept thy person? saith the Lord of hosts."

5. Psalm 51:17: "The sacrifices of God are a broken spirit: a broken and a contrite heart, O God, thou wilt not despise."

6. Isaiah 1:11-17: These verses criticize offerings made without true repentance and righteousness, emphasizing God's desire for genuine worship.

7. Ephesians 4:26-27: "Be ye angry, and sin not: let not the sun go down upon your wrath: Neither give place to the devil."

8. James 1:19-20: "Wherefore, my beloved brethren, let every man be swift to hear, slow to speak, slow to wrath: For the wrath of man worketh not the righteousness of God."

Provision and Abundance:

- Provision: Both Cain and Abel brought offerings from their respective labors, indicating that God had provided them with the means to work and produce. This provision allowed them to bring gifts to God as acts of worship.

- Abundance: Abel's offering of the firstlings and the fat portions signifies giving from abundance and prioritizing God with the best. This reflects an attitude of gratitude and recognition of God's provision.

Application:

- Heart of Worship: The difference in God's response to Cain and Abel's offerings highlights the importance of the heart and attitude behind our acts of worship. Genuine faith and devotion are key (Hebrews 11:4).

- Responsibility and Response: Cain's anger and fallen countenance serve as a warning about how we respond to correction and rejection. Addressing underlying issues and maintaining a right heart attitude is crucial (Ephesians 4:26-27).

- Quality of Offerings: Giving our best to God, as Abel did, signifies honoring Him with our first and finest, reflecting our gratitude and reverence (Proverbs 3:9-10).

God's Plan for Resource Management and Human Attitudes

1. God's Continued Provision:

"Every moving thing that liveth shall be meat for you; even as the green herb have I given you all things." (Genesis 9:3, KJV)

Interpretation:

In this verse, God grants humanity the permission to eat all living creatures, expanding their diet beyond the green plants that were initially given to them in the Garden of Eden.

This verse marks a significant shift in the dietary regulations for humanity following the flood.

Commentary:

"Every moving thing that liveth shall be meat for you": This phrase indicates a new provision from God, allowing humans to eat animals. Previously, in Genesis 1:29-30, the diet of humans was restricted to plants. The post-flood world introduces a broader dietary allowance, including all living creatures (Genesis 1:29-30).

"Even as the green herb have I given you all things": This comparison to the green plants emphasizes that just as plants were given for food, now all animals are also provided for sustenance. It reflects God's provision and care for human needs, allowing a more diverse diet to sustain life (Genesis 1:29; Psalm 104:14-15).

Concordance:

- Every moving thing that liveth shall be meat for you: This phrase signifies God's expanded provision for human diet, allowing the consumption of animals (Leviticus 11:2; Deuteronomy 14:4-5).

- Even as the green herb have I given you all things: This statement reflects God's initial provision of plants for food and now includes animals, showing the comprehensive nature of God's provision (Genesis 1:29; Psalm 104:14-15).

References from the King James Bible:

1. Genesis 1:29-30: "And God said, Behold, I have given you every herb bearing seed, which is upon the face of all the earth, and every tree, in the which is the fruit of a tree yielding seed; to you it shall be for meat. And to every beast of the earth, and to every fowl of the air, and to every thing that creepeth upon the earth, wherein there is life, I have given every green herb for meat: and it was so."

2. Leviticus 11:2: "Speak unto the children of Israel, saying, These are the beasts which ye shall eat among all the beasts that are on the earth."

3. Deuteronomy 14:4-5: "These are the beasts which ye shall eat: the ox, the sheep, and the goat, The hart, and the roebuck, and the fallow deer, and the wild goat, and the pygarg, and the wild ox, and the chamois."

4. Psalm 104:14-15: "He causeth the grass to grow for the cattle, and herb for the service of man: that he may bring forth food out of the earth; And wine that maketh glad the heart of man, and oil to make his face to shine, and bread which strengtheneth man's heart."

Provision and Abundance:

- Provision: God's allowance for humans to eat animals in addition to plants shows His provision for their nutritional needs in a post-flood world. This provision ensures that humanity has adequate food sources.
- Abundance: The inclusion of "every moving thing that liveth" indicates an abundant provision, granting humans access to a wide variety of foods. This highlights God's generosity and care in providing sustenance.

Application:

- Gratitude for Provision: Recognizing that all food, whether plant or animal, is a gift from God should inspire gratitude. Every meal is a reminder of God's care and provision.

- Responsibility in Stewardship: While God grants humans the right to eat animals, this comes with the responsibility of ethical treatment and stewardship of God's creation. Responsible and sustainable practices reflect respect for God's provision.

- Understanding Shifts in Divine Instructions: The shift from a plant-based diet to including animals shows God's adaptability in meeting human needs. Understanding these changes helps in interpreting the broader narrative of God's relationship with humanity.

2. The Call to Stewardship:

Verse 2: "And I will make of thee a great nation, and I will bless thee, and make thy name great; and thou shalt be a blessing." (Genesis 12:2, KJV)

Verse 3: "And I will bless them that bless thee, and curse him that curseth thee: and in thee shall all families of the earth be blessed." (Genesis 12:3, KJV)

Interpretation:

In these verses, God speaks to Abram (later Abraham), promising to make him into a great nation, to bless him, and to make his name great. Abram is also called to be a blessing to others. Furthermore, God promises to bless those who bless Abram and to curse those who curse him. The ultimate promise is that all families of the earth will be blessed through Abram, pointing to the coming of the Messiah and the universal blessing through Jesus Christ.

Commentary:

Verse 2:

"And I will make of thee a great nation, and I will bless thee, and make thy name great; and thou shalt be a blessing."

- "And I will make of thee a great nation": God promises Abram that his descendants will become a great nation. This is the beginning of the covenant promise that Abram's offspring would be numerous and significant (Genesis 17:4-6; Exodus 1:7).

- "And I will bless thee": This blessing includes prosperity, protection, and divine favor. God's blessing is comprehensive, impacting all areas of Abram's life (Genesis 24:1; Deuteronomy 28:2-6).

- "And make thy name great": Abram's name will be renowned and honored. This promise is fulfilled as Abram becomes Abraham, the patriarch of the Israelites, and a key figure in the three major monotheistic religions (Genesis 17:5; Nehemiah 9:7).

- "And thou shalt be a blessing": Abram is not only to be blessed but also to be a source of blessing to others. His life and legacy will positively impact the world, particularly through his descendants (Galatians 3:14).

Verse 3:

"And I will bless them that bless thee, and curse him that curseth thee: and in thee shall all families of the earth be blessed."

- "And I will bless them that bless thee, and curse him that curseth thee": God promises to protect Abram and his descendants by blessing those who support them and cursing those who oppose them. This establishes a divine principle of reciprocal treatment (Numbers 24:9; Isaiah 41:11-12).

- "And in thee shall all families of the earth be blessed": This is the ultimate promise that points to the global impact of Abram's lineage, culminating in the coming of Jesus Christ. Through Christ, all nations and peoples are offered salvation and blessing (Galatians 3:8, 16).

Concordance:

- Great nation: God's promise to make Abram's descendants a great nation (Genesis 17:4-6; Exodus 1:7).

- Blessing: The comprehensive nature of God's blessing on Abram (Genesis 24:1; Deuteronomy 28:2-6).

- Name great: The renown and honor of Abram's name (Genesis 17:5; Nehemiah 9:7).

- Reciprocal treatment: God's protection of Abram through blessings and curses (Numbers 24:9; Isaiah 41:11-12).

- Global blessing: The universal impact of Abram's lineage, especially through Christ (Galatians 3:8, 16).

References from the King James Bible:

1. Genesis 17:4-6: "As for me, behold, my covenant is with thee, and thou shalt be a father of many nations. Neither shall thy name anymore be called Abram, but thy name shall be Abraham; for a father of many nations have I made thee. And I will make thee exceeding fruitful, and I will make nations of thee, and kings shall come out of thee."

2. Exodus 1:7: "And the children of Israel were fruitful, and increased abundantly, and multiplied, and waxed exceeding mighty; and the land was filled with them."

3. Genesis 24:1: "And Abraham was old, and well stricken in age: and the Lord had blessed Abraham in all things."

4. Deuteronomy 28:2-6: "And all these blessings shall come on thee, and overtake thee, if thou shalt hearken unto the voice of the Lord thy God. Blessed shalt thou be in the city, and blessed shalt thou be in the field. Blessed shall be the fruit of thy body, and the fruit of thy ground, and the fruit of thy cattle, the increase of thy kine, and the flocks of thy sheep. Blessed shall be thy basket and thy store. Blessed shalt thou be when thou comest in, and blessed shalt thou be when thou goest out."

5. Nehemiah 9:7: "Thou art the Lord the God, who didst choose Abram, and broughtest him forth out of Ur of the Chaldees, and gavest him the name of Abraham."

6. Numbers 24:9: "He couched, he lay down as a lion, and as a great lion: who shall stir him up? Blessed is he that blesseth thee, and cursed is he that curseth thee."

7. Isaiah 41:11-12: "Behold, all they that were incensed against thee shall be ashamed and confounded: they shall be as nothing; and they that strive with thee shall perish. Thou shalt seek them, and shalt not find them, even them that contended with thee: they that war against thee shall be as nothing, and as a thing of nought."

8. Galatians 3:8: "And the scripture, foreseeing that God would justify the heathen through faith, preached before the gospel unto Abraham, saying, In thee shall all nations be blessed."

9. Galatians 3:16: "Now to Abraham and his seed were the promises made. He saith not, And to seeds, as of many; but as of one, And to thy seed, which is Christ."

Provision and Abundance:

- Provision: God's promise to bless Abram includes providing for his needs and ensuring his prosperity. This provision extends to his descendants and includes protection and favor.

- Abundance: The blessings promised to Abram are abundant, including becoming a great nation, having a great name, and being a source of blessing to others. The ultimate abundance is seen in the promise that all families of the earth will be blessed through Abram's lineage, fulfilled in Jesus Christ.

Application:

- Faith and Obedience: Abram's faith and obedience to God's call are exemplary. Believers are encouraged to trust in God's promises and follow His guidance, knowing that He is faithful to fulfill His word.

- Blessing Others: As recipients of God's blessings, believers are called to be a blessing to others. This involves sharing the love, grace, and truth of God with those around us.

- Global Perspective: The promise that all families of the earth will be blessed through Abram points to the global mission of the Church. Believers are called to share the Gospel and make disciples of all nations, extending God's blessing to the world.

Compliance of Adam and Eve with God's Plan

1. Initial Compliance:

"And they were both naked, the man and his wife, and were not ashamed." (Genesis 2:25, KJV)

Interpretation:

In this verse, the Bible describes the state of Adam and Eve before the Fall. Their nakedness signifies their innocence and purity. They were free from shame and guilt, living in perfect harmony with each other and with God.

Commentary:

"And they were both naked, the man and his wife": This phrase emphasizes the innocence and natural state of Adam and Eve. Their nakedness is symbolic of their transparency, openness, and lack of self-consciousness. In their pre-Fall state, they experienced no shame or guilt, reflecting a perfect and unbroken relationship with God and each other (Genesis 3:7, 10-11).

"And were not ashamed": The absence of shame indicates that Adam and Eve were free from sin and its consequences. They lived in a state of perfect innocence and trust, without fear or insecurity. This contrasts sharply with the post-Fall condition, where shame and guilt become part of the human experience (Genesis 3:7-8).

Concordance:

- Naked: The concept of nakedness in the Bible often symbolizes innocence or vulnerability. In this context, it signifies the purity and openness of the first humans before sin entered the world (Genesis 3:7, 10-11; Isaiah 47:3; Revelation 3:18).

- Not ashamed: The absence of shame points to a state of innocence and purity. It reflects the ideal state of human relationships and communion with God, which is marred by sin after the Fall (Genesis 3:7-8; Psalm 25:2-3; Romans 5:5).

References from the King James Bible:

1. Genesis 3:7: "And the eyes of them both were opened, and they knew that they were naked; and they sewed fig leaves together, and made themselves aprons."

2. Genesis 3:10-11: "And he said, I heard thy voice in the garden, and I was afraid, because I was naked; and I hid myself. And he said, Who told thee that thou wast naked? Hast thou eaten of the tree, whereof I commanded thee that thou shouldest not eat?"

3. Isaiah 47:3: "Thy nakedness shall be uncovered, yea, thy shame shall be seen: I will take vengeance, and I will not meet thee as a man."

4. Revelation 3:18: "I counsel thee to buy of me gold tried in the fire, that thou mayest be rich; and white raiment, that thou mayest be clothed, and that the shame of thy

nakedness do not appear; and anoint thine eyes with eyesalve, that thou mayest see."

5. Psalm 25:2-3: "O my God, I trust in thee: let me not be ashamed, let not mine enemies triumph over me. Yea, let none that wait on thee be ashamed: let them be ashamed which transgress without cause."

6. Romans 5:5: "And hope maketh not ashamed; because the love of God is shed abroad in our hearts by the Holy Ghost which is given unto us."

Provision and Abundance:

- Provision: God's creation provided a perfect environment for Adam and Eve, where they lacked nothing and were in complete harmony with each other and with God. Their nakedness without shame reflects the abundance of God's provision in their lives.

- Abundance: The state of being unashamed indicates the abundance of peace, trust, and innocence in their relationship. There was no fear, guilt, or need for pretense, highlighting the richness of their original condition.

Application:

- Innocence and Trust: The nakedness and lack of shame in Adam and Eve's pre-Fall state serve as a model for innocence, openness, and trust in relationships. Believers are called to strive for honesty and transparency in their relationships with God and others.

- Consequences of Sin: The contrast between the pre-Fall and post-Fall states underscores the devastating impact of sin on human relationships and self-perception. Recognizing this can deepen our understanding of the need for redemption and restoration through Christ.

- Restoration through Christ: The absence of shame in the pre-Fall state points to the restoration that is possible through Christ. Believers can experience freedom from guilt and shame through the forgiveness and new life offered in Jesus (Romans 8:1).

2. Disobedience and Its Consequences:

- Genesis 3:6: "And when the woman saw that the tree was good for food, and that it was pleasant to the eyes, and a tree to be desired to make one wise, she took of the fruit thereof, and did eat, and gave also unto her husband with her; and he did eat." (Genesis 3:6, KJV)

Interpretation:

In this verse, Eve succumbs to the temptation presented by the serpent. She sees the tree's fruit as good for food, attractive, and desirable for gaining wisdom. After eating the fruit, she gives some to Adam, who also eats. This act of disobedience leads to the Fall of humanity.

Commentary:

"And when the woman saw that the tree was good for food": Eve's temptation begins with a focus on the physical appeal of the fruit. It looked good for eating, appealing to the appetite and physical desires (1 John 2:16).

"And that it was pleasant to the eyes": The fruit was visually appealing, highlighting the allure of external appearances and the temptation that comes through what is seen (Proverbs 6:25).

"And a tree to be desired to make one wise": The promise of wisdom and enlightenment was a significant part of the temptation. The serpent's deception suggested that eating the fruit would elevate Eve's status and understanding (James 1:5).

"She took of the fruit thereof and did eat": Eve's decision to eat the fruit signifies the act of disobedience. This moment marks the first human sin, which is characterized by disobedience to God's direct command (Genesis 2:16-17).

"And gave also unto her husband with her; and he did eat": Adam's participation indicates that he was complicit in the act. Both Adam and Eve chose to disobey God, leading to the consequences of the Fall (Romans 5:12).

Concordance:

- Good for food: Physical desires and appetites can lead to temptation (1 John 2:16; Matthew 4:3).
- Pleasant to the eyes: Visual allure can be a source of temptation (Proverbs 6:25; 1 John 2:16).
- Desired to make one wise: The desire for wisdom and status can lead to temptation (James 1:5; 1 Corinthians 3:18).
- Disobedience: The act of taking and eating the fruit represents disobedience to God's command (Genesis 2:16-17; Romans 5:12).

References from the King James Bible:

1. 1 John 2:16: "For all that is in the world, the lust of the flesh, and the lust of the eyes, and the pride of life, is not of the Father, but is of the world."

2. Proverbs 6:25: "Lust not after her beauty in thine heart; neither let her take thee with her eyelids."

3. James 1:5: "If any of you lack wisdom, let him ask of God, that giveth to all men liberally, and upbraideth not; and it shall be given him."

4. 1 Corinthians 3:18: "Let no man deceive himself. If any man among you seemeth to be wise in this world, let him become a fool, that he may be wise."

5. Genesis 2:16-17: "And the Lord God commanded the man, saying, Of every tree of the garden thou mayest freely eat: But of the tree of the knowledge of good and evil, thou shalt not eat of it: for in the day that thou eatest thereof thou shalt surely die."

6. Romans 5:12: "Wherefore, as by one man sin entered into the world, and death by sin; and so death passed upon all men, for that all have sinned."

7. Matthew 4:3: "And when the tempter came to him, he said, If thou be the Son of God, command that these stones be made bread."

Provision and Abundance:

- Provision: Before the Fall, God had provided Adam and Eve with everything they needed, including a variety of food sources. Their decision to eat from the forbidden tree was not out of necessity but out of a desire for what was not theirs to take (Genesis 1:29-30).

- Abundance: God's provision in the Garden of Eden was abundant, with many trees bearing good fruit. The act of eating from the forbidden tree indicates a lack of contentment with God's abundant provision and a desire for more (Genesis 2:9).

Application:

- Guarding Against Temptation: The narrative of Eve's temptation underscores the importance of being vigilant against the various forms of temptation that appeal to physical desires, visual allure, and the desire for status or wisdom.

- Obedience to God's Word: The disobedience of Adam and Eve serves as a stark reminder of the importance of adhering to God's commands. Trusting in God's provision and wisdom is crucial for maintaining a right relationship with Him.

- Consequences of Sin: The immediate consequences of Adam and Eve's actions highlight the serious nature of sin. Their disobedience led to the Fall, affecting all of humanity. This emphasizes the need for redemption and the hope found in Christ (Romans 5:18-19).

Lessons from Genesis on Money and Resources

1. Trust in God's Provision:
- Genesis 22:14: "And Abraham called the name of that place Jehovahjireh: as it is said to this day, In the mount of the Lord it shall be seen." (Genesis 22:14, KJV)

Interpretation:

In this verse, Abraham names the location where God provided a ram as a substitute sacrifice for his son Isaac "Jehovahjireh," meaning "The Lord Will Provide." This name commemorates God's provision and foreshadows His ultimate provision in Jesus Christ. The phrase "In the mount of the Lord it shall be seen" suggests that God's provision will be evident on this mountain.

Commentary:

"And Abraham called the name of that place Jehovahjireh": The name "Jehovahjireh" (YHWH Yireh) means "The Lord Will Provide." This name reflects Abraham's faith and gratitude for God's provision of a ram to be sacrificed in place of Isaac. It signifies God's foresight and provision for the needs of His people (Genesis 22:8).

"As it is said to this day, In the mount of the Lord it shall be seen": This phrase indicates that the location became a significant site remembered for God's provision. The phrase "it shall be seen" can also be translated as "it shall be provided," underscoring the belief that God's provision would continue to be evident at this place. This location is traditionally identified with Mount Moriah, which is later associated with the Temple Mount in Jerusalem, linking it to future acts of divine provision, including the sacrifice of Jesus Christ (2 Chronicles 3:1).

Concordance:

- Jehovahjireh: This name for God emphasizes His role as a provider. It is one of the compound names of God in the Old Testament, highlighting His attributes and actions (Exodus 3:14; Psalm 23:1).

- Mount of the Lord: Refers to a place where God's presence and provision are particularly evident. This phrase connects to significant locations of worship and divine encounters in the Bible (Exodus 3:1-2; Isaiah 2:3).

References from the King James Bible:

1. Genesis 22:8: "And Abraham said, My son, God will provide himself a lamb for a burnt offering: so they went both of them together."

2. Exodus 3:14: "And God said unto Moses, I AM THAT I AM: and he said, Thus shalt thou say unto the children of Israel, I AM hath sent me unto you."

3. Psalm 23:1: "The Lord is my shepherd; I shall not want."

4. 2 Chronicles 3:1: "Then Solomon began to build the house of the Lord at Jerusalem in mount Moriah, where the Lord appeared unto David his father, in the place that David had prepared in the threshingfloor of Ornan the Jebusite."

5. Exodus 3:1-2: "Now Moses kept the flock of Jethro his father-in-law, the priest of Midian: and he led the flock to the backside of the desert, and came to the mountain of God, even to Horeb. And the angel of the Lord appeared unto him in a flame of fire out of the midst of a bush: and he looked, and, behold, the bush burned with fire, and the bush was not consumed."

6. Isaiah 2:3: "And many people shall go and say, Come ye, and let us go up to the mountain of the Lord, to the house of the God of Jacob; and he will teach us of his ways, and we will walk in his paths: for out of Zion shall go forth the law, and the word of the Lord from Jerusalem."

Provision and Abundance:

- Provision: God provided a ram as a substitute for Isaac, demonstrating His care and provision for Abraham and his family. This event foreshadows God's ultimate provision of Jesus Christ as the Lamb of God who takes away the sin of the world (John 1:29).

- Abundance: The name Jehovahjireh reflects the abundance of God's provision, not only in meeting immediate needs but also in the larger redemptive plan. God's provision is both immediate and eternal, encompassing all aspects of life and salvation (Philippians 4:19).

Application:

- Faith in God's Provision: Abraham's naming of the place Jehovahjireh encourages believers to trust in God's provision. Even in times of testing and uncertainty, God is faithful to provide for His people (Romans 8:32).

- Recognition of God's Hand: Naming places of significant spiritual encounters helps to remember and recognize God's hand in our lives. It serves as a testimony to others of God's faithfulness and provision (Joshua 4:6-7).

- Foreshadowing Christ's Sacrifice: The provision of the ram as a substitute for Isaac points to Jesus Christ, the ultimate provision for humanity's salvation. This encourages believers to see the Old Testament as foreshadowing the redemptive work of Christ (Hebrews 11:17-19).

2. Generosity and Sacrifice:
- Genesis 14:19-20:
Verse 19: "And he blessed him, and said, Blessed be Abram of the most high God, possessor of heaven and earth:" (Genesis 14:19, KJV)

Verse 20: "And blessed be the most high God, which hath delivered thine enemies into thy hand. And he gave him tithes of all." (Genesis 14:20, KJV)

Interpretation:

In these verses, Melchizedek, the king of Salem and a priest of the Most High God, blesses Abram. Melchizedek acknowledges God as the possessor of heaven and earth and attributes Abram's victory over his enemies to God's intervention. In response, Abram gives Melchizedek a tenth of all the spoils, recognizing his priestly authority and God's provision.

Commentary:

Verse 19:
"And he blessed him, and said, Blessed be Abram of the most high God, possessor of heaven and earth:"

- "And he blessed him": Melchizedek, both a king and a priest, blesses Abram. This blessing is significant as it comes from a figure who represents both royal and priestly authority (Hebrews 7:1-2).

- "Blessed be Abram of the most high God": This phrase acknowledges Abram's relationship with God, indicating that his blessings come from the Most High God, El Elyon. It signifies divine favor upon Abram (Genesis 12:2-3).

- "Possessor of heaven and earth": Melchizedek identifies God as the sovereign owner of all creation. This recognition of God's ultimate authority underscores the source of Abram's victory and blessings (Psalm 24:1).

Verse 20:

"And blessed be the most high God, which hath delivered thine enemies into thy hand. And he gave him tithes of all."

- "And blessed be the most high God": Melchizedek continues by blessing God, acknowledging His power and sovereignty in granting Abram victory. This emphasizes that Abram's success is due to divine intervention (Daniel 4:34-35).

- "Which hath delivered thine enemies into thy hand": This phrase highlights that it was God's power that enabled

Abram to defeat his enemies. It points to God's role as a deliverer and protector of His people (Psalm 18:48).

- "And he gave him tithes of all": In response to Melchizedek's blessing and acknowledgment of God's sovereignty, Abram gives him a tenth of the spoils. This act of giving a tithe recognizes Melchizedek's priestly role and shows gratitude to God for His provision (Hebrews 7:4-10).

Concordance:

- Blessing: The act of blessing is significant in biblical texts, often indicating divine favor and approval (Genesis 12:2-3; Numbers 6:24-26).

- Most High God (El Elyon): This name of God emphasizes His supremacy and sovereignty over all creation (Psalm 7:17; Daniel 4:34-35).

- Tithes: The giving of tithes, or a tenth, is a practice of acknowledging God's provision and sovereignty, often associated with worship and gratitude (Leviticus 27:30; Malachi 3:10).

References from the King James Bible:

1. Genesis 12:2-3: "And I will make of thee a great nation, and I will bless thee, and make thy name great; and thou shalt be a blessing: And I will bless them that bless thee, and curse him that curseth thee: and in thee shall all families of the earth be blessed."

2. Psalm 24:1: "The earth is the Lord's, and the fulness thereof; the world, and they that dwell therein."

3. Hebrews 7:1-2: "For this Melchisedec, king of Salem, priest of the most high God, who met Abraham returning from the slaughter of the kings, and blessed him; To whom also Abraham gave a tenth part of all; first being by interpretation King of righteousness, and after that also King of Salem, which is, King of peace;"

4. Daniel 4:34-35: "And at the end of the days I Nebuchadnezzar lifted up mine eyes unto heaven, and mine understanding returned unto me, and I blessed the most High, and I praised and honoured him that liveth for ever, whose dominion is an everlasting dominion, and his kingdom is from generation to generation: And all the inhabitants of the earth are reputed as nothing: and he doeth according to his will in the army of heaven, and among the inhabitants of the earth: and none can stay his hand, or say unto him, What doest thou?"

5. Psalm 18:48: "He delivereth me from mine enemies: yea, thou liftest me up above those that rise up against me: thou hast delivered me from the violent man."

6. Leviticus 27:30: "And all the tithe of the land, whether of the seed of the land, or of the fruit of the tree, is the Lord's: it is holy unto the Lord."

7. Malachi 3:10: "Bring ye all the tithes into the storehouse, that there may be meat in mine house, and prove me now herewith, saith the Lord of hosts, if I will not open you the windows of heaven, and pour you out a blessing, that there shall not be room enough to receive it."

Provision and Abundance:

- Provision: Melchizedek's blessing highlights God's provision in Abram's victory. God is recognized as the one who delivers enemies into Abram's hand, emphasizing divine intervention and support.

- Abundance: The giving of tithes from Abram to Melchizedek reflects an acknowledgment of God's abundant blessings. It is an act of worship and gratitude for God's generous provision.

Application:

- Recognition of God's Sovereignty: Believers are called to recognize and acknowledge God's sovereignty over all aspects of life. Melchizedek's blessing of God as the possessor of heaven and earth serves as a reminder of God's ultimate authority.

- Gratitude and Worship: Abram's act of giving tithes reflects a heart of gratitude and worship. Believers are encouraged to respond to God's blessings with acts of worship and giving, acknowledging His provision and sovereignty.

- Faith and Dependence on God: Abram's victory and subsequent blessing underscore the importance of faith and dependence on God. Success and deliverance come from God's hand, and recognizing this fosters a deeper trust and reliance on Him.

Conclusion

The book of Genesis provides foundational insights into the theology of money and resource management. God's plan for humanity includes responsible stewardship, generosity, and reliance on divine provision. While Adam and

Eve initially complied with God's plan, their disobedience introduced challenges in managing resources.

The narratives in Genesis highlight the importance of maintaining a proper attitude towards resources, emphasizing trust in God, ethical stewardship, and the impact of generosity. By understanding and applying these principles, believers can align their financial practices with God's design, fostering a life of faithful stewardship and blessing to others.

CHAPTER 03

POLITICS OF MONEY IN THEOLOGY

Money, with its capacity to influence individuals and societies, occupies a central place in both secular politics and theological discourse. The intersection of money and politics, especially within a theological framework, raises profound questions about morality, justice, and stewardship. This chapter explores the politics of money in theology, examining biblical teachings and their implications for contemporary socio-economic and political structures.

The Love of Money and its Consequences

1. The Root of All Evil:

- 1 Timothy 6:10: "For the love of money is a root of all kinds of evil. Some people, eager for money, have wandered from the faith and pierced themselves with many griefs."

- Commentary: This verse highlights the corrupting influence of money when it becomes an object of obsessive desire. The love of money can lead to ethical compromises, social injustices, and spiritual downfall. Theological teachings warn against the pursuit of wealth at the expense of faith and moral integrity.

Money and Power

1. Wealth and Authority:

- Ecclesiastes 5:19: "Moreover, when God gives someone wealth and possessions, and the ability to enjoy them, to accept their lot and be happy in their toil—this is a gift of God."

- Commentary: While wealth itself is not condemned, it is portrayed as a gift from God, to be enjoyed responsibly. This verse suggests that wealth, when viewed as a divine blessing, should be used wisely and ethically, recognizing the responsibility that comes with it.

2. Economic Inequality:

- James 2:6: "But you have dishonored the poor. Is it not the rich who are exploiting you? Are they not the ones who are dragging you into court?"

- Commentary: James criticizes the exploitation and oppression of the poor by the wealthy. This criticism extends to contemporary socio-economic systems where wealth disparities lead to injustice and exploitation. The verse calls for a re-evaluation of economic policies and practices that perpetuate inequality.

Justice and Fairness in Economic Practices

1. Honest Weights and Measures:

- Proverbs 11:1: "The Lord detests dishonest scales, but accurate weights find favor with him."

- Commentary: This proverb emphasizes the importance of honesty and fairness in economic transactions. It underscores the ethical imperative for just business practices, advocating for integrity and transparency in all financial dealings.

2. Wages and Labor:

- James 5:4: "Look! The wages you failed to pay the workers who mowed your fields are crying out against you. The cries of the harvesters have reached the ears of the Lord Almighty."

- Commentary: This verse condemns the exploitation of labor and the withholding of fair wages. It highlights the divine concern for justice in employment practices and the moral duty to treat workers fairly. Theological perspectives advocate for economic systems that ensure fair compensation and dignified working conditions.

Generosity and Stewardship

1. Generosity to the Poor:
- Proverbs 19:17: "Whoever is kind to the poor lends to the Lord, and he will reward them for what they have done."

- Commentary: This verse encourages generosity and compassion towards the poor, framing it as an act of service to God. The theological imperative to care for the less fortunate challenges individuals and communities to prioritize charitable giving and social responsibility.

2. Parable of the Talents:

- Matthew 25:14-30: The parable tells of a master who entrusts his servants with varying amounts of money and rewards them based on their stewardship.

- Commentary: This parable illustrates the principles of stewardship and accountability. It teaches that wealth and resources are to be managed wisely and used for the greater good. The servants' differing outcomes reflect the importance of responsible and proactive management of what is entrusted to us.

Wealth, Politics, and the Kingdom of God

1. Render unto Caesar:

- Matthew 22:21: "Then he said to them, 'So give back to Caesar what is Caesar's, and to God what is God's.'"

- Commentary: Jesus' teaching here addresses the relationship between secular authority and divine obligation. It implies a distinction between political and spiritual responsibilities, suggesting that while participating in civic duties, one must also fulfill spiritual commitments. This verse informs the debate on the appropriate interaction between faith and politics, especially regarding financial obligations and taxation.

2. The Rich Young Ruler:

- Mark 10:21-22: "Jesus looked at him and loved him. 'One thing you lack,' he said. 'Go, sell everything you have and give to the poor, and you will have treasure in heaven. Then come, follow me.'"

- Commentary: The story of the rich young ruler highlights the tension between wealth and discipleship. Jesus' call to sell possessions and give to the poor underscores the radical commitment required to follow Him. It challenges believers to consider how their wealth influences their spiritual priorities and engagement with the Kingdom of God.

Addressing Modern Economic Challenges

1. Advocacy for Economic Justice:

- Micah 6:8: "He has shown you, O mortal, what is good. And what does the Lord require of you? To act justly and to love mercy and to walk humbly with your God."

- Commentary: This verse encapsulates the divine mandate for justice, mercy, and humility. It calls for active engagement in promoting economic justice, addressing systemic inequalities, and advocating for policies that reflect these values.

2. Global Solidarity:

- Galatians 3:28: "There is neither Jew nor Gentile, neither slave nor free, nor is there male and female, for you are all one in Christ Jesus."

- Commentary: This verse emphasizes the unity and equality of all people in Christ. It challenges economic systems that perpetuate divisions and inequalities, advocating for a global perspective that recognizes the interconnectedness of all humanity.

Conclusion

The politics of money in theology addresses the profound ethical and moral questions surrounding wealth, power, and economic practices. Biblical teachings provide a framework for understanding the responsibilities and challenges associated with wealth, and advocating for justice, fairness, and compassion. By integrating these principles into contemporary socio-economic structures, faith communities can work towards a more just and equitable society, reflecting the values of the Kingdom of God. As we navigate the complexities of money and politics, these theological insights offer guidance and inspiration for transformative action.

CHAPTER 04

ECOLOGY OF MONEY

The concept of the "ecology of money" explores the intricate relationships between financial systems, environmental sustainability, and ethical stewardship. Understanding how money flows through economies and impacts the environment is crucial for creating a sustainable future. This chapter examines the biblical principles that guide our financial decisions and their ecological implications, offering a framework for aligning economic practices with environmental stewardship.

The Earth as God's Creation

1. Stewardship of Creation:

- Genesis 2:15: "The Lord God took the man and put him in the Garden of Eden to work it and take care of it."

- Commentary: From the beginning, humanity was entrusted with the responsibility to care for God's creation. This foundational principle of stewardship underscores the importance of managing the Earth's resources wisely and sustainably.

2. Creation's Goodness:

- Genesis 1:31: "God saw all that he had made, and it was very good."

- Commentary: The inherent goodness of creation reflects God's craftsmanship and intention. Our financial systems and economic activities should honor this goodness by promoting practices that protect and preserve the environment.

The Impact of Economic Activities on the Environment

1. Environmental Degradation:

- Isaiah 24:5-6: "The earth is defiled by its people; they have disobeyed the laws, violated the statutes and broken the everlasting covenant. Therefore, a curse consumes the earth; its people must bear their guilt."

- Commentary: Isaiah's prophecy highlights the consequences of humanity's disregard for God's laws, including environmental degradation. Modern economic activities that exploit natural resources and pollute the environment reflect this broken covenant, calling for a return to responsible stewardship.

2. Responsible Use of Resources:

- Proverbs 12:10: "The righteous care for the needs of their animals, but the kindest acts of the wicked are cruel."

- Commentary: This proverb underscores the importance of compassionate and ethical treatment of all creation. Sustainable economic practices that minimize harm to the environment and living beings align with biblical righteousness.

Sustainable and Ethical Financial Practices

1. Ethical Investments:

- Matthew 6:19-20: "Do not store up for yourselves treasures on earth, where moths and vermin destroy, and where thieves break in and steal. But store up for yourselves treasures in heaven, where moths and vermin do not destroy, and where thieves do not break in and steal."

- Commentary: Jesus' teaching encourages investing in what is eternal and of lasting value. Ethical investments that support environmental sustainability and social justice reflect this principle, prioritizing long-term well-being over short-term gains.

2. Green Finance:

- Psalm 24:1: "The earth is the Lord's, and everything in it, the world, and all who live in it."

- Commentary: Recognizing that the Earth belongs to God calls us to manage its resources with respect and care. Green finance, which includes investments in renewable energy, conservation, and sustainable practices, honors this divine ownership.

Economic Justice and Environmental Stewardship

1. Justice for the Poor:

- Proverbs 14:31: "Whoever oppresses the poor shows contempt for their Maker, but whoever is kind to the needy honors God."

- Commentary: Economic systems that exploit the poor and degrade the environment show contempt for God's creation. Just economic practices that uplift the poor and protect the environment honor God and reflect His love for all creation.

2. Fair Trade:

- James 5:4: "Look! The wages you failed to pay the workers who mowed your fields are crying out against you. The cries of the harvesters have reached the ears of the Lord Almighty."

- Commentary: This verse condemns the exploitation of workers and calls for fair compensation. Fair trade practices ensure that producers receive just wages and work in safe conditions, promoting both economic justice and environmental sustainability.

The Role of Faith Communities in Promoting Sustainable Economics

1. Advocacy and Education:

- Micah 6:8: "He has shown you, O mortal, what is good. And what does the Lord require of you? To act justly and to love mercy and to walk humbly with your God."

- Commentary: Faith communities are called to advocate for justice and educate their members about sustainable economic practices. By raising awareness and promoting ethical consumption, they can influence broader societal changes towards sustainability.

2. Community Initiatives:

- Acts 4:32: "All the believers were one in heart and mind. No one claimed that any of their possessions was their own, but they shared everything they had."

- Commentary: The early Christian community's example of sharing resources reflects a model of economic solidarity and mutual support. Faith communities today can initiate projects that promote sustainability, such as community gardens, recycling programs, and support for local, sustainable businesses.

Integrating Theology and Economics

1. Holistic Stewardship:

- Colossians 1:16: "For in him all things were created: things in heaven and on earth, visible and invisible, whether thrones or powers or rulers or authorities; all things have been created through him and for him."

- Commentary: This verse reminds us that all of creation belongs to Christ and exists for His glory. Integrating theology and economics involves recognizing the sacredness of all creation and ensuring that our economic activities reflect this understanding.

2. Living Out the Kingdom of God:

- Matthew 6:33: "But seek first his kingdom and his righteousness, and all these things will be given to you as well."

- Commentary: Seeking God's kingdom involves prioritizing righteousness and justice in all areas of life, including our economic decisions. By aligning our financial practices with the values of God's kingdom, we contribute to a more just and sustainable world.

Conclusion

The ecology of money calls for a re-examination of how our financial systems and economic activities impact the environment and society. Biblical principles provide a framework for sustainable and ethical financial practices that honor God's creation and promote justice. By integrating these principles into our economic decisions, we can work towards a future where money serves as a tool for stewardship, justice, and the flourishing of all creation. As we continue to explore the theology of money, the interconnections between economics, ecology, and ethics become ever more apparent, guiding us toward a holistic approach to financial stewardship.

CHAPTER 05

MONEY IN RELIGIOUS TEXTS

Money and wealth have always been central themes in religious texts, shaping various faith traditions' ethical and moral frameworks. This chapter explores how different religious scriptures portray money, examining their guidance on economic matters, and the moral and ethical lessons they convey about wealth and its use.

Money in the Bible

The Bible, both in the Old and New Testaments, addresses money and wealth extensively:

1. Old Testament:

- Proverbs and Ecclesiastes: These wisdom books provide numerous insights on money. Proverbs 3:9-10 emphasizes honoring God with wealth and receiving blessings in return. Ecclesiastes 5:10 warns that loving money leads to dissatisfaction, stating, "Whoever loves money never has enough; whoever loves wealth is never satisfied with their income."

- The Law of Moses: The Torah includes various laws about money, such as prohibitions against usury (Exodus 22:25) and mandates for fair treatment of the poor and just economic practices (Leviticus 19:13, Deuteronomy 15:7-8).

2. New Testament:

- Jesus' Teachings: Jesus spoke frequently about money, often highlighting the spiritual dangers of wealth. In Matthew 6:24, He states, "No one can serve two masters... You cannot serve both God and money." The parable of the rich fool (Luke 12:16-21) and the story of the rich young ruler (Mark 10:17-27) underscore the potential for wealth to impede spiritual growth.

- The Early Church: Acts 4:32-35 describes the early Christian community's practice of sharing possessions and wealth, emphasizing communal support and the redistribution of resources.

My primary objective in these messages is to convey insights into God's economy. Let us examine 1 Timothy 1:3-7: "I urge you, as I did when I was going to Macedonia, to remain in Ephesus so that you may instruct certain people not to teach any different doctrine, nor to occupy themselves with myths and endless genealogies that promote speculations rather than the divine training that is known by faith. The aim of such instruction is love that comes from a pure heart, a good conscience, and sincere faith. Some people have deviated from these and turned to meaningless talk, desiring to be teachers of the law, without understanding either what they are saying or the things about which they make assertions."

God's Plan and Missing the Mark

The Apostle Paul was specifically chosen by God to oversee His divine plan and he trained his spiritual son, Timothy, in this divine enterprise. Paul's epistle to Timothy was written during a period when many Christians had deviated from the original path, missing the central mark of God's plan and focusing on other things.

Distractions from God's Plan

Historically, two predominant influences led early Christians astray: Judaism and Gnosticism. The Judaizers, with their strict adherence to religious doctrines and forms, and the Gnostics, with their philosophical inclinations, both diverted the believers from the path of God's plan. The Mosaic Law, while inherently good and divinely instituted, became a distraction when it overshadowed the essence of God's plan. Similarly, Gnostic philosophies, although beneficial to heathen civilizations, were misapplied within the church, steering believers away from God's central purpose.

Modern Distractions

Even today, despite the absence of Judaizers and Gnostics, numerous factors continue to distract us from God's plan. The subtle enemy has consistently used seemingly good aspects of Christianity to divert believers from following the Lord on the correct path. Many well-meaning religious activities and scriptural interpretations have been manipulated to distract God's children from His plan.

Defining God's Plan

What precisely is God's plan? A thorough and spiritually insightful study of the Scriptures reveals that God's plan is fundamentally His design to dispense Himself into humanity. This divine dispensation involves God distributing Himself into the human race. Unfortunately, the term "dispensation" has been misconstrued within Christianity, often referring to different periods of God's administrative arrangements. However, in the context of God's plan, it signifies God's intent to dispense His essence into us.

God's Capital and Business

God, in His boundless richness, can be likened to a prosperous businessman with immense capital. His enterprise in this universe involves dispensing Himself—His very essence—into humanity. This requires a divine arrangement, systematic management, and an efficient dispensation to facilitate this process.

Understanding God's Substance

To comprehend what God is dispensing, we must understand His substance. God's essence is Spirit (John 4:24).

He intends to reproduce Himself through the mass production of this spiritual substance, free of charge, to humanity.

The Triune God: Steps of Dispensation

God's plan is actualized through the Trinity: the Father, the Son, and the Holy Spirit. While the concept of the Trinity has been extensively discussed in Christianity, it can only be fully understood in the context of divine dispensation. The Trinity's purpose is to serve as the means through which God's Spirit is dispensed into humanity.

The Process of Dispensation

2 Corinthians 13:14 outlines the stages of God's plan through the Trinity: "The grace of the Lord Jesus Christ, and the love of God, and the fellowship of the Holy Spirit, be with you all." Here, love is the source, grace is the expression of love, and fellowship is the transmission of this love in grace. God, Christ, and the Holy Spirit represent one God in three Persons: God is the source, Christ is the expression, and the Holy Spirit is the transmission bringing God in Christ into

man. This divine process involves three successive stages: from the Father, in the Son, and through the Spirit.

From the Father

God the Father is the universal source, invisible and unapproachable. To make Himself accessible, He embodied Himself in the Son. All the fullness of the Father dwells in the Son and is expressed through Him. The previously inaccessible God is now approachable through the Son.

In the Son

The second stage involves the Son, in whom seven essential elements are mingled: divine nature, human nature, daily human life with its sufferings, the effectiveness of His death, resurrection power, ascension, and enthronement. These elements combined constitute the all-inclusive Christ.

Through the Spirit

The final stage involves the Spirit, who, after the Lord's ascension, encompasses all the elements of Christ. This all-inclusive Spirit, who indwells and encompasses us, enables the mingling of God with man. The Holy Spirit is the reality of Christ, who imparts life, liberty, and transformation into our being, fulfilling the goal of God's plan.

The ultimate aim of God's plan is to dispense Himself into us, facilitating a transformative mingling with His divine essence. By focusing on this divine plan and not being sidetracked by doctrinal distractions, we partake in the fullness of God's dispensation, living by the Triune God who dwells within our human spirit.

Money in the Quran

The Quran offers a comprehensive framework for economic conduct, blending spiritual and practical guidance:

1. Wealth as a Trust: The Quran views wealth as a trust from Allah, to be used responsibly. Surah Al-Baqarah (2:261) compares charitable giving to a grain that sprouts into seven ears, each bearing a hundred grains, emphasizing the multiplied rewards of generosity.

- Zakat (Almsgiving): One of the Five Pillars of Islam, Zakat is an obligatory act of charity. Surah At-Tawbah

(9:60) outlines the recipients of Zakat, underscoring its role in alleviating poverty and promoting social justice.

- Prohibition of Riba (Usury): The Quran strictly forbids usury, considering it exploitative. Surah Al-Baqarah (2:275-276) states, "Allah has permitted trade and forbidden usury," and warns of severe consequences for those who engage in it.

Money in Hindu Scriptures

Hinduism, with its diverse array of texts and traditions, also addresses money and wealth:

1. Dharma and Artha: The concept of Purusharthas outlines four goals of human life, including Artha (wealth). Hindu texts like the Arthashastra and the Manusmriti discuss the ethical acquisition and use of wealth within the framework of Dharma (moral duty).

- Bhagavad Gita: The Gita discusses detachment from material wealth and the importance of performing one's duties without selfish desire. In Chapter 2, Verse 47, Krishna advises Arjuna, "You have a right to perform your prescribed duties, but you are not entitled to the fruits of your actions."

Money in Buddhist Texts

Buddhist teachings offer a nuanced perspective on money and wealth, focusing on ethical conduct and the alleviation of suffering:

1. Right Livelihood: One of the steps on the Noble Eightfold Path, Right Livelihood, encourages earning a living in a way that does not harm others. The Digha Nikaya emphasizes avoiding occupations that involve harm, deceit, or exploitation.

- Generosity (Dana): Generosity is a fundamental virtue in Buddhism. The Jataka tales and the Pali Canon recount numerous stories highlighting the importance of selfless giving and the cultivation of a compassionate heart.

Money in Judaic Texts

Judaism provides detailed teachings on economic justice and the ethical use of wealth:

1. Tzedakah (Charity): Rooted in the Torah, Tzedakah is a religious obligation, promoting social justice and the support of the needy. Deuteronomy 15:7-8 urges generosity

towards the poor, reflecting the communal responsibility to aid those in need.

- Business Ethics: The Talmud offers extensive guidance on fair business practices, honest trade, and the ethical treatment of workers, emphasizing integrity and justice in economic dealings.

Conclusion

Religious texts offer a rich tapestry of teachings on money and wealth, each providing unique ethical and moral perspectives. These teachings underscore the importance of using wealth responsibly, promoting social justice, and prioritizing spiritual well-being over material gain. As we continue to explore the theology of money, these foundational perspectives will inform our understanding of contemporary economic practices and their alignment with religious values.

CHAPTER 06

THE MONETARY LIFE OF JOB – A THEOLOGICAL
PERSPECTIVE

The Book of Job is a profound exploration of human suffering, divine sovereignty, and the complexity of faith. While it primarily addresses the question of why the righteous suffer, it also offers rich insights into the monetary life of Job, providing a theological framework for understanding wealth, loss, and restoration from a biblical perspective. This chapter delves into Job's financial experiences, examining how his wealth, losses, and eventual restoration fit within a theological context.

Job's Initial Wealth

1. Abundant Prosperity:

- Job 1:1-3: "In the land of Uz there lived a man whose name was Job. This man was blameless and upright; he feared God and shunned evil. He had seven sons and three daughters, and he owned seven thousand sheep, three thousand camels, five hundred yoke of oxen and five hundred donkeys, and had a large number of servants. He was the greatest man among all the people of the East."

- Commentary: Job's initial wealth is described in great detail, emphasizing his vast possessions and high status. His prosperity is portrayed as a sign of God's blessing, reflecting the biblical principle that righteousness often leads to material blessings (Proverbs 10:22).

The Loss of Wealth

1. Sudden Calamity:

- Job 1:13-19: In a series of rapid, devastating events, Job loses all his wealth and children. Raiders steal his livestock, fire consumes his sheep, and a mighty wind destroys the house where his children were feasting.

- Commentary: The sudden and total loss of Job's wealth serves as a dramatic reversal of his fortunes. It challenges the simplistic equation of righteousness with prosperity, highlighting the vulnerability of even the most blessed individuals to suffering and loss.

2. Job's Response to Loss:

- Job 1:20-21: "At this, Job got up and tore his robe and shaved his head. Then he fell to the ground in worship and said: 'Naked I came from my mother's womb, and naked I will depart. The Lord gave and the Lord has taken away; may the name of the Lord be praised.'"

- Commentary: Job's response to his financial and personal losses is one of profound faith and submission to God's sovereignty. He acknowledges that all he had was given by God and that God has the right to take it away. This response sets a theological precedent for viewing wealth as ultimately belonging to God and underscores the importance of worship and trust in God over material possessions.

Theological Reflections on Wealth and Suffering

1. Wealth and Righteousness:

- Job 1:8: "Then the Lord said to Satan, 'Have you considered my servant Job? There is no one on earth like him; he is blameless and upright, a man who fears God and shuns evil.'"

- Commentary: Job's wealth is initially associated with his righteousness. However, the book of Job complicates this association by demonstrating that righteousness does not guarantee continued prosperity. Instead, it emphasizes that faithfulness to God transcends material conditions.

2. The Role of Suffering:

- Job 2:9-10: "His wife said to him, 'Are you still maintaining your integrity? Curse God and die!' He replied, 'You are talking like a foolish woman. Shall we accept good from God, and not trouble?' In all this, Job did not sin in what he said."

- Commentary: Job's steadfastness in the face of suffering challenges the notion that prosperity is the ultimate sign of God's favor. His acceptance of both good and bad from God reflects a deep theological understanding of God's sovereignty and the complexity of the human experience.

Dialogues on Wealth and Justice

1. Eliphaz's Perspective:

- Job 4:7-8: "Consider now: Who, being innocent, has ever perished? Where were the upright ever destroyed? As

I have observed, those who plow evil and those who sow trouble reap it."

- Commentary: Eliphaz's argument reflects a common theological perspective that suffering is a direct result of personal sin. However, the book of Job ultimately rejects this simplistic view, demonstrating that the relationship between righteousness, wealth, and suffering is more nuanced.

2. Job's Defense:

- Job 29:12-17: "Because I rescued the poor who cried for help, and the fatherless who had none to assist them. The one who was dying blessed me; I made the widow's heart sing. I put on righteousness as my clothing; justice was my robe and my turban. I was eyes to the blind and feet to the lame. I was a father to the needy; I took up the case of the stranger. I broke the fangs of the wicked and snatched the victims from their teeth."

- Commentary: Job defends his integrity and righteousness, highlighting his just and compassionate use of wealth. This passage underscores the biblical ideal that wealth should be used to promote justice and support the vulnerable, aligning with the broader scriptural mandate for economic justice (Proverbs 31:8-9).

Restoration and Divine Justice

1. Job's Restoration:

- Job 42:10-12: "After Job had prayed for his friends, the Lord restored his fortunes and gave him twice as much as he had before. All his brothers and sisters and everyone who had known him before came and ate with him in his house. They comforted and consoled him over all the trouble the Lord had brought on him, and each one gave him a piece of silver and a gold ring. The Lord blessed the latter part of Job's life more than the former part. He had fourteen thousand sheep, six thousand camels, a thousand yoke of oxen and a thousand donkeys."

- Commentary: The restoration of Job's wealth and fortunes underscores the theme of divine justice and mercy. However, the restoration is not simply a return to previous conditions but an indication of God's abundant grace. This conclusion reinforces the idea that while wealth can be a sign of God's blessing, true prosperity lies in a restored relationship with God.

Lessons from Job's Monetary Life

1. Transient Nature of Wealth:

- Ecclesiastes 5:15: "Everyone comes naked from their mother's womb, and as everyone comes, so they depart. They take nothing from their toil that they can carry in their hands."

- Commentary: Job's experience highlights the transient nature of wealth and the importance of holding material possessions loosely. True security and worth are found in one's relationship with God, not in material wealth.

2. Faithfulness in Prosperity and Adversity:

- Philippians 4:12-13: "I know what it is to be in need, and I know what it is to have plenty. I have learned the secret of being content in any and every situation, whether well fed or hungry, whether living in plenty or in want. I can do all this through him who gives me strength."

- Commentary: Job's unwavering faith amidst drastic changes in his financial status exemplifies the attitude Paul describes. Believers are called to be content and faithful, whether in times of abundance or scarcity, relying on God's strength.

Conclusion

The monetary life of Job provides a profound theological exploration of wealth, loss, and restoration. Through his experiences, we learn that wealth is a gift from God to be stewarded with justice and compassion, but it is not the ultimate measure of divine favor. The book of Job challenges us to maintain our integrity and faith in God regardless of our material circumstances, understanding that true prosperity is found in a faithful relationship with the Creator. As we navigate our own financial journeys, the lessons from Job's life offer timeless wisdom and guidance.

CHAPTER 07

THE MONETARY LIFE OF KING SOLOMON – A THEOLOGICAL PERSPECTIVE

King Solomon, renowned for his wisdom, wealth, and extensive building projects, is one of the most significant figures in biblical history. His reign represents the zenith of Israel's prosperity and influence. This chapter explores the theological dimensions of Solomon's monetary life, examining his wealth, the spiritual implications of his relationship with God, and the lessons we can learn from his life.

Solomon's Divine Wisdom and Wealth

1. God's Gift of Wisdom and Wealth:

- 1 Kings 3:12-13: "I will give you a wise and discerning heart so that there will never have been anyone like you, nor will there ever be. Moreover, I will give you what you have not asked for—both wealth and honor—so that in your lifetime you will have no equal among kings."

- Commentary: Solomon's wealth and wisdom were divine gifts, granted in response to his humble request for discernment to govern God's people. This passage underscores the principle that true wisdom and prosperity come from God and are to be used in service to Him and His people.

The Extent of Solomon's Wealth

1. Unparalleled Prosperity:

- 1 Kings 10:14-15: "The weight of the gold that Solomon received yearly was 666 talents, not including the revenues from merchants and traders and from all the Arabian kings and the governors of the territories."

- Commentary: Solomon's annual income from gold alone was immense, highlighting the extraordinary wealth accumulated during his reign. His prosperity was a testament to God's blessing and the fulfillment of divine promises.

2. Magnificent Projects:

- 1 Kings 6:1-2: "In the four hundred and eightieth year after the Israelites came out of Egypt, in the fourth year of Solomon's reign over Israel, in the month of Ziv, the second month, he began to build the temple of the Lord. The temple that King Solomon built for the Lord was sixty cubits long, twenty wide, and thirty high."

- Commentary: Solomon's wealth enabled him to undertake grand projects, including the construction of the temple in Jerusalem. This temple became the central place of worship for Israel, symbolizing God's presence among His people. Solomon's dedication to building the temple reflects his initial commitment to using his wealth for God's glory.

Solomon's Wisdom and Economic Policies

1. Economic Strategies:

- 1 Kings 10:23-24: "King Solomon was greater in riches and wisdom than all the other kings of the earth. The whole world sought audience with Solomon to hear the wisdom God had put in his heart."

- Commentary: Solomon's wisdom attracted international attention, leading to trade agreements and alliances that further enriched Israel. His ability to manage resources and engage in diplomacy was a reflection of God's wisdom at work through him.

2. Social and Economic Impact:

- 1 Kings 4:25: "During Solomon's lifetime Judah and Israel, from Dan to Beersheba, lived in safety, everyone under their own vine and under their own fig tree."

- Commentary: Solomon's reign brought unprecedented peace and prosperity to Israel. The imagery of each person living under their own vine and fig tree symbolizes economic stability and individual prosperity, resulting from wise and just governance.

The Spiritual Decline of Solomon

1. Idolatry and Apostasy:

- 1 Kings 11:4: "As Solomon grew old, his wives turned his heart after other gods, and his heart was not fully devoted to the Lord his God, as the heart of David his father had been."

- Commentary: Despite his wisdom and wealth, Solomon's heart was led astray by his foreign wives, who introduced idolatry into Israel. His spiritual decline serves as a cautionary tale about the dangers of wealth and power without steadfast devotion to God.

2. Consequences of Disobedience:

- 1 Kings 11:11: "So the Lord said to Solomon, 'Since this is your attitude and you have not kept my covenant and my decrees, which I commanded you, I will most certainly tear the kingdom away from you and give it to one of your subordinates.'"

- Commentary: Solomon's failure to remain faithful to God had severe consequences for his kingdom. This passage highlights the principle that obedience to God is paramount, and deviation from His commands leads to downfall and division.

Theological Lessons from Solomon's Life

1. The Source of True Wisdom:

- Proverbs 2:6: "For the Lord gives wisdom; from his mouth come knowledge and understanding."

- Commentary: Solomon's wisdom was a gift from God, reminding us that true wisdom originates from the divine. Believers are encouraged to seek God's guidance and wisdom in all aspects of life, including financial decisions.

2. The Dangers of Wealth and Power:

- Matthew 6:24: "No one can serve two masters. Either you will hate the one and love the other, or you will be devoted to the one and despise the other. You cannot serve both God and money."

- Commentary: Solomon's life illustrates the potential for wealth and power to lead one away from God. Jesus' teaching reinforces the need for a singular devotion to God, warning against the divided loyalties that wealth can create.

3. The Importance of Heart Devotion:

- Proverbs 4:23: "Above all else, guard your heart, for everything you do flows from it."

- Commentary: Solomon's downfall began with his heart's departure from God. This verse emphasizes the need to guard our hearts diligently, ensuring that our devotion remains steadfast and undivided.

Spiritual Insights from Solomon's Relationship with God

1. God's Faithfulness and Human Frailty:

- 1 Kings 9:4-5: "As for you, if you walk before me faithfully with integrity of heart and uprightness, as David your father did, and do all I command and observe my decrees and laws, I will establish your royal throne over Israel forever, as I promised David your father."

- Commentary: God's promises to Solomon were contingent on his faithfulness. This conditionality underscores the dynamic relationship between divine sovereignty and human responsibility. While God remains faithful, human frailty can hinder the fulfillment of divine promises.

2. The Legacy of Wisdom:

- Ecclesiastes 12:13: "Now all has been heard; here is the conclusion of the matter: Fear God and keep his commandments, for this is the duty of all mankind."

- Commentary: Traditionally attributed to Solomon, Ecclesiastes concludes with a powerful reminder of the centrality of fearing God and keeping His commandments. This legacy of wisdom calls believers to prioritize their relationship with God above all else.

Conclusion

The monetary life of King Solomon offers profound theological insights into the interplay between wealth, wisdom, and spiritual devotion. Solomon's life exemplifies the potential for great prosperity and the dangers of spiritual complacency. His initial dedication to using his wealth for God's glory, followed by his eventual spiritual decline, serves as a timeless reminder of the importance of maintaining a heart fully devoted to God.

From Solomon's relationship with God, we learn that true wisdom and prosperity come from divine gifts, and their proper use requires unwavering commitment to God's commandments. The lessons from Solomon's life call us to seek divine wisdom, guard our hearts, and use our resources to honor God and promote justice. By integrating these principles into our lives, we can navigate the complexities of wealth and power with faithfulness and integrity, reflecting the values of God's kingdom.

CHAPTER 08

THE ALL-SUFFICIENT SPIRIT

The focus of this chapter is on the all-sufficient Spirit, which is essential in God's economy. God, in His divine arrangement, dispenses Himself into humanity, transforming and renewing us through the Spirit.

The Indwelling Spirit

The indwelling of the Holy Spirit is a fundamental concept in the economy of God. John 14:16-17 states, "And I will ask the Father, and he will give you another Advocate, to be with you forever. This is the Spirit of truth, whom the world cannot receive because it neither sees him nor knows him. You know him because he abides with you, and he will be in you." The Spirit not only dwells with us but also resides within us, making God's presence a constant reality in our lives.

The Function of the Spirit

The primary function of the Spirit is to impart the divine life into our being. Romans 8:10-11 says, "But if Christ is in you, though the body is dead because of sin, the Spirit is life because of righteousness. If the Spirit of him who raised Jesus from the dead dwells in you, he who raised Christ from the dead will give life to your mortal bodies also through his Spirit that dwells in you." This life-giving aspect of the Spirit transforms us from within, making us partakers of the divine nature.

The Transforming Work of the Spirit

The Spirit's work is not limited to imparting life; it also involves transformation. 2 Corinthians 3:18 explains, "And all of us, with unveiled faces, seeing the glory of the Lord as though reflected in a mirror, are being transformed into the same image from one degree of glory to another; for this comes from the Lord, the Spirit." This transformation process aligns us with the image of Christ, changing our inner being to reflect His glory.

The Fellowship of the Spirit

The Spirit also facilitates fellowship among believers. Philippians 2:1-2 mentions, "If then there is any encouragement in Christ, any consolation from love, any sharing in the Spirit, any compassion and sympathy, make my joy complete: be of the same mind, having the same love, being in full accord and of one mind." The fellowship of the Spirit brings unity and harmony within the body of Christ, enabling us to live and function as one.

The Spirit's Sufficiency

The Spirit is all-sufficient, providing everything we need for our spiritual growth and development. Galatians 5:22-23 lists the fruit of the Spirit, "By contrast, the fruit of the Spirit is love, joy, peace, patience, kindness, generosity, faithfulness, gentleness, and self-control. There is no law against such things." These attributes reflect the sufficiency of the Spirit in producing a Christ-like character within us.

The all-sufficient Spirit is central to God's economy. By indwelling, transforming, and uniting us, the Spirit accomplishes God's purpose of dispensing Himself into humanity. This divine economy ensures that we are continually being conformed to the image of Christ, living in the fullness of God's life and power.

John 3:6 tells us, "That which is born of the Spirit is spirit." This verse highlights two distinct "spirits": one is the Holy Spirit of God, and the other is the human spirit of man. The divine Spirit brings new birth to our human spirit, signifying the profound indwelling of God's presence within us.

The Human Spirit and the Divine Spirit

The interplay between the human spirit and the Holy Spirit is central to our spiritual life. John 4:24 emphasizes, "God is Spirit, and those who worship Him must worship in spirit and truth." This demonstrates the necessity of engaging our human spirit in genuine worship, aligned with God's Spirit.

Indwelling of the Triune God

Romans 8:16 further affirms, "The Spirit Himself bears witness with our spirit that we are children of God." This mutual indwelling ensures a continuous, intimate relationship with God. Our human spirit becomes the residence for the Holy Spirit, marking us as God's children and enabling us to experience His divine life.

The Function of the Spirit

The Spirit's role extends beyond mere indwelling. It encompasses guidance, transformation, and empowerment. As 1 Corinthians 6:17 states, "But he who is joined to the Lord is one spirit with Him." This union illustrates the profound integration of the divine and human spirits, resulting in a life led by God's Spirit.

The Tabernacle as a Symbol

The structure of the Old Testament tabernacle, with its three parts—the outer court, the holy place, and the Holiest of all—parallels our tripartite being: body, soul, and spirit. Just as God's presence dwelled in the innermost part of the Tabernacle, so does the Holy Spirit reside in our human spirit, the deepest part of our being.

The Practical Experience of the Indwelling Spirit

Practically experiencing the indwelling Spirit involves recognizing and responding to His presence within us. This entails daily fellowship, prayer, and yielding to His guidance. By doing so, we allow the Holy Spirit to permeate every aspect of our lives, transforming us into the likeness of Christ.

The All-Sufficient Spirit

The Holy Spirit is sufficient to meet all our needs. He provides wisdom, strength, comfort, and guidance. As we grow in our relationship with the Spirit, we experience the fullness of God's provision, enabling us to live victorious and fruitful lives.

The residence of the Divine Spirit in our human spirit is a cornerstone of God's economy. This indwelling facilitates an intimate relationship with God, guiding us into all truth and transforming our lives. By embracing the Holy Spirit's presence, we fulfill God's purpose of dispensing Himself into humanity, living as true children of God.

The essence of the Christian life hinges on understanding and experiencing the indwelling Spirit. This chapter delves into the significance and practical aspects of having the Holy Spirit dwell within us, guiding our daily lives and spiritual growth.

The Indwelling Spirit's Role

The indwelling Spirit plays a critical role in God's economy. According to Romans 8:9, "But you are not in the flesh; you are in the Spirit, if in fact the Spirit of God dwells in you. Anyone who does not have the Spirit of Christ does not belong to him." This verse underscores the necessity of the Holy Spirit's presence in distinguishing those who belong to Christ.

Experiencing the Indwelling Spirit

The experience of the indwelling Spirit begins with the new birth. John 3:5-6 states, "Jesus answered, 'Very truly, I tell you, no one can enter the kingdom of God without being born of water and Spirit. What is born of the flesh is flesh, and what is born of the Spirit is spirit.'" This birth initiates the indwelling of the Holy Spirit, making us new creations in Christ.

The Spirit's Transformative Power

The transformative power of the Spirit is evident in the renewal of our minds and hearts. Romans 12:2 exhorts, "Do not be conformed to this world, but be transformed by the renewing of your minds, so that you may discern what is the will of God—what is good and acceptable and perfect." This transformation aligns us with God's will, reshaping our thoughts and behaviors.

The Practical Outworking of the Spirit

Practically, the indwelling Spirit guides us in all truth and empowers us to live righteously. John 16:13 says, "When the Spirit of truth comes, he will guide you into all the truth; for he will not speak on his own, but will speak whatever he hears, and he will declare to you the things that are to come." This guidance is essential for navigating life according to God's purposes.

The Spirit as Our Comforter

The Holy Spirit also functions as our Comforter. John 14:16-17 reveals, "And I will ask the Father, and he will give you another Advocate, to be with you forever. This is the Spirit of truth, whom the world cannot receive, because it neither sees him nor knows him. You know him, because he abides with you, and he will be in you." The Spirit provides comfort, reassurance, and strength, especially in times of difficulty.

Maintaining Fellowship with the Spirit

Maintaining a vibrant relationship with the Holy Spirit requires continual fellowship. Ephesians 6:18 advises, "Pray in the Spirit at all times in every prayer and supplication. To that end, keep alert and always persevere in supplication for all the saints." Prayer and supplication in the Spirit keep us connected to God and sensitive to His leading.

The Outcome of the Indwelling Spirit

The outcome of having the indwelling Spirit is a life marked by spiritual fruitfulness. Galatians 5:22-23 lists the fruit of the Spirit as "love, joy, peace, patience, kindness, generosity, faithfulness, gentleness, and self-control. There is no law against such things." These qualities reflect the character of Christ and are evidence of the Spirit's work within us.

Conclusion

Understanding and experiencing the indwelling Spirit is crucial to fulfilling God's economy. By allowing the Holy Spirit to transform, guide, comfort, and maintain fellowship with us, we live out the reality of God's presence within. This divine indwelling enables us to manifest the life of Christ and accomplish God's purpose in and through us.

CHAPTER 09

THE THEOLOGY OF MONEY IN THE LIFE OF JESUS

The life and teachings of Jesus Christ provide profound insights into the theology of money. Throughout His ministry, Jesus addressed the use, value, and dangers of wealth, offering a divine perspective on how believers should relate to money. This chapter explores the theology of money in the life of Jesus, examining His teachings, actions, and the implications for contemporary Christian practice.

Jesus' Early Life and Economic Background

1. Humble Beginnings:
    - Luke 2:7: "She wrapped him in cloths and placed him in a manger, because there was no guest room available for them."

- Commentary: Jesus' birth in a manger reflects His humble beginnings and the modest economic status of His earthly family. This setting underscores the theme of humility and God's identification with the poor and marginalized.

2. Carpenter's Son:

- Mark 6:3: "Isn't this the carpenter? Isn't this Mary's son and the brother of James, Joseph, Judas and Simon? Aren't his sisters here with us?"

- Commentary: Jesus grew up in a working-class family, learning the trade of carpentry. His background as a carpenter's son highlights the value of honest labor and the dignity of work, irrespective of economic status.

Jesus' Teachings on Wealth and Possessions

1. The Sermon on the Mount:

- Matthew 6:19-21: "Do not store up for yourselves treasures on earth, where moths and vermin destroy, and where thieves break in and steal. But store up for yourselves treasures in heaven, where moths and vermin do not destroy, and where thieves do not break in and steal. For where your treasure is, there your heart will be also."

- Commentary: Jesus warns against the accumulation of earthly wealth, emphasizing the transient nature of material possessions. He encourages His followers to invest in eternal treasures, which reflect one's true priorities and spiritual focus.

2. The Rich Young Ruler:

- Mark 10:21-22: "Jesus looked at him and loved him. 'One thing you lack,' he said. 'Go, sell everything you have and give to the poor, and you will have treasure in heaven. Then come, follow me.' At this the man's face fell. He went away sad, because he had great wealth."

- Commentary: The encounter with the rich young ruler illustrates the challenge of wealth in following Jesus. The young man's attachment to his possessions prevented him from fully committing to discipleship, highlighting the potential spiritual hindrance of material wealth.

3. Parable of the Rich Fool:

- Luke 12:16-21: "And he told them this parable: 'The ground of a certain rich man yielded an abundant harvest. He thought to himself, "What shall I do? I have no place to store my crops." Then he said, "This is what I'll do. I will tear down my barns and build bigger ones, and there I will store my surplus grain. And I'll say to myself, "You have plenty of grain laid up for many years. Take life easy; eat, drink and be merry." But God said to him, "You fool! This very night your life will be demanded from you. Then who will get what you have prepared for yourself?" This is how it will be with whoever stores up things for themselves but is not rich toward God.'"

   - Commentary: The parable of the rich fool warns against hoarding wealth and living selfishly. It underscores the futility of placing security in material possessions and the importance of being "rich toward God" through generosity and reliance on divine provision.

Jesus' Actions and Attitudes Towards Money

1. The Cleansing of the Temple:
   - Matthew 21:12-13: "Jesus entered the temple courts and drove out all who were buying and selling there. He overturned the tables of the money changers and the benches of those selling doves. 'It is written,' he said to them, 'My house will be called a house of prayer, but you are making it a den of robbers.'"

   - Commentary: Jesus' cleansing of the temple reflects His condemnation of commercial exploitation within a sacred space. It emphasizes the sanctity of worship and the need to prioritize spiritual integrity over financial gain.

2. Dependence on Divine Provision:

- Matthew 17:24-27: When asked about the temple tax, Jesus instructs Peter to catch a fish, in which he finds a coin to pay the tax for both of them.

- Commentary: This miracle demonstrates Jesus' teaching on reliance on God's provision. It highlights that God can provide for material needs in unexpected ways, encouraging believers to trust in divine providence rather than earthly wealth.

The Role of Money in Jesus' Ministry

1. Support from Followers:

- Luke 8:1-3: "After this, Jesus traveled about from one town and village to another, proclaiming the good news of the kingdom of God. The Twelve were with him, and also some women who had been cured of evil spirits and diseases: Mary (called Magdalene) from whom seven demons had come out; Joanna the wife of Chuza, the manager of Herod's household; Susanna; and many others. These women were helping to support them out of their own means."

- Commentary: Jesus' ministry was supported financially by His followers, including women of means. This support underscores the importance of stewardship and generosity in advancing God's kingdom.

2. Judas and the Betrayal:

- Matthew 26:14-16: "Then one of the Twelve—the one called Judas Iscariot—went to the chief priests and asked, 'What are you willing to give me if I deliver him over to you?' So they counted out for him thirty pieces of silver. From then on Judas watched for an opportunity to hand him over."

- Commentary: The betrayal of Jesus by Judas for thirty pieces of silver highlights the corrupting power of money. It serves as a stark reminder of how greed can lead to moral failure and the ultimate tragedy.

Theological Implications and Lessons

1. Generosity and Selflessness:

- Acts 20:35: "In everything I did, I showed you that by this kind of hard work we must help the weak, remembering the words the Lord Jesus himself said: 'It is more blessed to give than to receive.'"

- Commentary: Jesus' teaching emphasizes the blessedness of generosity. Christians are called to adopt a posture of selflessness and to use their resources to support and uplift others.

2. Trust in God's Provision:

- Matthew 6:31-33: "So do not worry, saying, 'What shall we eat?' or 'What shall we drink?' or 'What shall we wear?' For the pagans run after all these things, and your heavenly Father knows that you need them. But seek first his kingdom and his righteousness, and all these things will be given to you as well."

- Commentary: Jesus encourages His followers to prioritize seeking God's kingdom and righteousness over material concerns. This teaching reassures believers of God's awareness and provision for their needs.

3. Detachment from Material Wealth:

- Matthew 19:23-24: "Then Jesus said to his disciples, 'Truly I tell you, it is hard for someone who is rich to enter the kingdom of heaven. Again I tell you, it is easier for a camel to go through the eye of a needle than for someone who is rich to enter the kingdom of God.'"

- Commentary: Jesus warns of the spiritual dangers associated with wealth. The challenge for the wealthy to enter the kingdom of God underscores the importance of detachment from material possessions and the need for humility and dependence on God.

Conclusion

The theology of money in the life of Jesus offers a counter-cultural perspective on wealth, generosity, and dependence on God. Jesus' teachings and actions consistently emphasize the transient nature of material possessions and the eternal value of spiritual riches. By studying His life, believers are encouraged to adopt attitudes of generosity, trust in divine provision, and detachment from wealth.

Jesus' relationship with money challenges contemporary Christians to evaluate their own attitudes towards wealth and possessions. His life and teachings call for a radical reorientation of values, prioritizing the kingdom of God and its righteousness above all else. As followers of Christ, we are invited to live out these principles, reflecting the heart of Jesus in our financial decisions and stewardship.

CHAPTER 10

THE THEOLOGY OF MONEY IN THE LIFE OF JOSEPH

The life of Joseph, as recorded in the book of Genesis, provides profound lessons on the theological understanding of money, stewardship, and God's providence. Joseph's journey from a favored son to a slave, and eventually to a powerful leader in Egypt, showcases his integrity, wisdom, and faithfulness in managing resources. This chapter explores the theological lessons from Joseph's life regarding money and how these lessons can be applied to our own financial practices.

Joseph's Early Life and God's Favor

1. God's Favor and Jealousy:

- Genesis 37:3-4: "Now Israel loved Joseph more than any of his other sons, because he had been born to him in his old age; and he made an ornate robe for him. When his brothers saw that their father loved him more than any of them, they hated him and could not speak a kind word to him."

- Commentary: Joseph's early life was marked by favoritism from his father, Jacob, which led to jealousy and hatred from his brothers. This familial conflict set the stage for Joseph's future trials and growth. It also highlights the importance of equitable treatment and the potential dangers of favoritism in financial matters.

2. Dreams of Greatness:

- Genesis 37:5-7: "Joseph had a dream, and when he told it to his brothers, they hated him all the more. He said to them, 'Listen to this dream I had: We were binding sheaves of grain out in the field when suddenly my sheaf rose and stood upright, while your sheaves gathered around mine and bowed down to it.'"

- Commentary: Joseph's dreams foreshadow his future rise to power and responsibility. These dreams, given by God, indicate His sovereign plan for Joseph's life, which includes significant financial and administrative responsibilities.

Joseph's Trials and Faithfulness

1. Sold into Slavery:

- Genesis 37:28: "So when the Midianite merchants came by, his brothers pulled Joseph up out of the cistern and sold him for twenty shekels of silver to the Ishmaelites, who took him to Egypt."

- Commentary: Joseph's sale into slavery represents a severe trial and a dramatic change in his financial and social status. Despite this injustice, Joseph's faith in God remains steadfast, demonstrating resilience and trust in God's providence.

2. Integrity in Potiphar's House:

- Genesis 39:4-6: "Joseph found favor in his eyes and became his attendant. Potiphar put him in charge of his household, and he entrusted to his care everything he owned. From the time he put him in charge of his household and of all that he owned the Lord blessed the household of the Egyptians because of Joseph. The blessing of the Lord was on everything Potiphar had, both in the house and in the field.

So, Potiphar left everything he had in Joseph's care; with Joseph in charge, he did not concern himself with anything except the food he ate."

- Commentary: In Potiphar's house, Joseph's integrity and competence lead to significant responsibility. His faithful management of Potiphar's resources results in blessings for the entire household, showcasing the theological principle that godly stewardship brings blessings to others.

Joseph's Rise to Power and Financial Management

1. Interpreting Pharaoh's Dreams:
- Genesis 41:15-16: "Pharaoh said to Joseph, 'I had a dream, and no one can interpret it. But I have heard it said of you that when you hear a dream you can interpret it.' 'I cannot do it,' Joseph replied to Pharaoh, 'but God will give Pharaoh the answer he desires.'"

- Commentary: Joseph's humility and reliance on God in interpreting Pharaoh's dreams emphasize that true wisdom and understanding come from God. This attitude is crucial for financial management, as it acknowledges divine guidance in making prudent decisions.

2. Preparation for Famine:

- Genesis 41:33-36: "And now let Pharaoh look for a discerning and wise man and put him in charge of the land of Egypt. Let Pharaoh appoint commissioners over the land to take a fifth of the harvest of Egypt during the seven years of abundance. They should collect all the food of these good years that are coming and store up the grain under the authority of Pharaoh, to be kept in the cities for food. This food should be held in reserve for the country, to be used during the seven years of famine that will come upon Egypt, so that the country may not be ruined by the famine."

- Commentary: Joseph's strategic planning during the years of abundance to prepare for the years of famine demonstrates prudent financial management and foresight. His actions highlight the importance of saving and resource management in anticipation of future needs, a key principle in financial stewardship.

Joseph's Generosity and Forgiveness

1. Provision for His Family:

- Genesis 45:7-8: "But God sent me ahead of you to preserve for you a remnant on earth and to save your lives by a great deliverance. So then, it was not you who sent me here, but God. He made me father to Pharaoh, lord of his entire household and ruler of all Egypt."

- Commentary: Joseph's recognition of God's sovereignty in his life and his provision for his family during the famine illustrate the theological principle of using one's resources to bless others, especially those in need. His forgiveness of his brothers and generosity towards them reflect a godly attitude towards wealth and reconciliation.

2. Sustaining Israel:

- Genesis 47:12: "Joseph also provided his father and his brothers and all his father's household with food, according to the number of their children."

- Commentary: Joseph's ongoing support for his family ensures their survival and prosperity in Egypt. This act of sustained generosity aligns with the biblical mandate to care for one's family and community, emphasizing the importance of using resources to support and sustain others.

Lessons from Joseph's Life on Money and Stewardship

1. Faithfulness in All Circumstances:

- Genesis 39:21-23: "The Lord was with him; he showed him kindness and granted him favor in the eyes of the prison warden. So, the warden put Joseph in charge of all those held in the prison, and he was made responsible for all that was done there. The warden paid no attention to anything under Joseph's care because the Lord was with Joseph and gave him success in whatever he did."

- Commentary: Joseph's faithfulness and integrity in all circumstances, whether in Potiphar's house, prison, or Pharaoh's court, highlight the importance of consistent godly stewardship. This principle applies to managing financial resources with integrity and faithfulness, regardless of one's situation.

2. Divine Providence and Human Responsibility:

- Genesis 50:20: "You intended to harm me, but God intended it for good to accomplish what is now being done, the saving of many lives."

- Commentary: Joseph's acknowledgment of God's providence in turning adverse circumstances into blessings illustrates the interplay between divine sovereignty and human responsibility. Understanding that God can work through difficult situations encourages believers to remain faithful and responsible stewards of their resources.

3. Wisdom in Resource Management:

- Genesis 41:39-40: "Then Pharaoh said to Joseph, 'Since God has made all this known to you, there is no one so discerning and wise as you. You shall be in charge of my palace, and all my people are to submit to your orders. Only with respect to the throne will I be greater than you.'"

- Commentary: Joseph's elevation to a position of significant authority due to his wisdom and discernment underscores the value of godly wisdom in financial and resource management. Believers are encouraged to seek divine wisdom in their financial decisions and stewardship practices.

Conclusion

The life of Joseph in the book of Genesis offers profound theological insights into money, stewardship, and God's providence. Joseph's journey from slavery to leadership exemplifies the importance of integrity, faithfulness, and wisdom in managing resources. His life teaches us to trust in God's providence, to be prudent in financial planning, and to use our resources to bless others.

By applying these lessons, believers can align their financial practices with biblical principles, ensuring that their stewardship honors God and serves His purposes. Joseph's example encourages us to remain faithful in all circumstances, to seek divine wisdom, and to use our resources for the greater good, reflecting God's love and generosity in our daily lives.

CHAPTER 11

ECONOMIC PHILOSOPHY AND THEOLOGY

The relationship between economic theories and theological principles is complex and multifaceted. Different belief systems offer distinct perspectives on wealth distribution, social justice, and economic behavior. This chapter examines how major economic philosophies intersect with theological principles, shaping societal views on wealth and justice.

2 Corinthians 4:3-7 states: "And even if our gospel is veiled, it is veiled to those who are perishing. In their case, the god of this world has blinded the minds of the unbelievers, to keep them from seeing the light of the gospel of the glory of Christ, who is the image of God. For we do not proclaim

ourselves; we proclaim Jesus Christ as Lord and ourselves as your slaves for Jesus' sake. For it is the God who said, 'Let light shine out of darkness,' who has shone in our hearts to give the light of the knowledge of the glory of God in the face of Jesus Christ. But we have this treasure in clay jars, so that it may be made clear that this extraordinary power belongs to God and does not come from us."

The Blinding of the Minds

Satan referred to as the god of this world, blinds the minds of unbelievers to prevent them from perceiving the light of the gospel. The enemy's strategy is to obscure the glory of Christ, thus hindering the understanding and acceptance of the divine truth.

The Treasure in Earthen Vessels

The gospel reveals that God's glory is manifest in the face of Jesus Christ. This divine glory, however, is housed in "earthen vessels"—our mortal bodies. The presence of this treasure within us demonstrates that the power and glory belong to God and not to ourselves.

God's Economy: Working Himself into Us

God's economy involves His intention to work Himself into humanity. This divine operation is carried out through His different Persons: the Father, the Son, and the Holy Spirit. Each Person of the Trinity plays a distinct role in this divine process, facilitating the infusion of God's essence into our being.

The Three Parts of Man

Man is created with three parts: spirit, soul, and body. This tripartite nature is crucial for understanding how God dispenses Himself into us. The spirit is the innermost part, the soul is the intermediary, and the body is the outermost part. God's work begins in our spirit and spreads to our soul and body.

The Triune God's Indwelling

Scripture shows that the Father, the Son, and the Holy Spirit each indwell the believers. Ephesians 4:6 mentions that God the Father is in us; 2 Corinthians 13:5 states that Jesus Christ is in us; and Romans 8:11 confirms that the Holy Spirit dwells in us. This indwelling of the Triune God forms the core of God's economy.

The Process of Dispensation

The process of God's dispensation involves the Father being embodied in the Son, and the Son being realized in the Spirit. The Father is the source, the Son is the embodiment and expression, and the Spirit is the realization and transmission of the Father and the Son into us.

The Spirit's Work in Man

The Holy Spirit's work begins with regeneration, transforming our spirit and making it alive with God's life. This regenerated spirit then becomes the base from which God spreads Himself into our soul and body. This spreading, or sanctification, gradually transforms our entire being, conforming us to the image of Christ.

The Persons of God and the parts of man are intricately connected in God's economy. Understanding this relationship is key to experiencing the fullness of God's life and presence within us. By allowing the Triune God to work

Himself into our spirit, soul, and body, we participate in the divine economy, fulfilling God's purpose for humanity.

Capitalism and Theology

Capitalism, characterized by private ownership and free markets, has both supporters and detractors within theological circles.

1. Proponents of Capitalism:
- Max Weber's Protestant Ethic: Max Weber argued that the Protestant work ethic, particularly Calvinist values of hard work and frugality, contributed to the development of capitalism. This ethic viewed economic success as a sign of divine favor.
- Prosperity Theology: Some Christian groups advocate for prosperity theology, which teaches that faith, positive speech, and donations to religious causes can increase one's material wealth. This perspective aligns closely with capitalist ideals of wealth accumulation.

2. Critics of Capitalism:
- Liberation Theology: Originating in Latin America, liberation theology criticizes capitalism for perpetuating

inequality and exploitation. It emphasizes the need for social justice and the preferential option for the poor, drawing on biblical themes of liberation and justice.

- Papal Encyclicals: Various papal encyclicals, such as Rerum Novarum (1891) and Laudato Si' (2015), critique the excesses of capitalism, advocating for economic systems that prioritize human dignity and the common good.

Socialism and Theology

Socialism advocates for collective ownership and distribution of resources, often aligning with theological principles that emphasize communal well-being and equality.

1. Christian Socialism:
- Historical Roots: Christian socialism emerged in the 19th century as a response to the injustices of industrial capitalism. It draws on biblical themes of community and justice, advocating for economic systems that reflect Christian ethics.

- Contemporary Views: Modern Christian socialists continue to call for economic reforms that address inequality and promote social justice, drawing inspiration from the early Christian community described in Acts 2:44-45.

2. Islamic Economic Principles:

- Zakat and Sadaqah: Islamic teachings on zakat (obligatory almsgiving) and sadaqah (voluntary charity) reflect a commitment to wealth redistribution and social welfare. These principles align with socialist ideals of economic justice and communal support.

- Prohibition of Riba: The prohibition of riba (usury) in Islamic finance promotes economic practices that avoid exploitation and ensure fairness, further aligning with socialist economic principles.

Economic Ethics in Hinduism and Buddhism

Hinduism and Buddhism offer unique perspectives on economic behavior, emphasizing ethical conduct and the moral implications of wealth.

1. Hindu Economic Thought:

- Dharma and Artha: Hindu philosophy integrates economic activity (artha) within the broader framework of dharma (moral duty). Wealth is seen as a legitimate pursuit, provided it is acquired and used ethically.

- Varna System: The traditional varna system, which divides society into different occupational classes, includes guidelines for ethical economic behavior, emphasizing the responsibilities of each class in maintaining social harmony.

2. Buddhist Economic Principles:

- Right Livelihood: As part of the Noble Eightfold Path, right livelihood encourages earning a living in ways that do not harm others. This principle advocates for ethical business practices and compassionate economic behavior.

- Sufficiency Economy: Inspired by Buddhist teachings, the sufficiency economy philosophy, promoted by Thailand's King Bhumibol Adulyadej, emphasizes moderation, self-reliance, and sustainable development.

Jewish Economic Ethics

Judaism offers a comprehensive framework for economic ethics, emphasizing justice, charity, and communal responsibility.

1. Tzedakah and Tikkun Olam:

- Tzedakah: The obligation of tzedakah (charity) is a central tenet of Jewish economic ethics, promoting the fair distribution of wealth and support for the needy.

- Tikkun Olam: The concept of tikkun olam (repairing the world) underscores the Jewish commitment to social justice and ethical conduct in economic activities.

2. Business Ethics:

- Honest Trade: Jewish law, as outlined in the Talmud, emphasizes honesty in business transactions, fair treatment of workers, and the prohibition of exploitative practices.

- Sabbatical and Jubilee Years: The biblical laws of the sabbatical year (Shmita) and the jubilee year (Yovel) reflect Jewish values of economic reset, debt forgiveness, and land redistribution, aiming to prevent long-term inequality and ensure social justice.

Accordingly, understanding the inward and hidden parts of our being is crucial for grasping how God works within us. These parts include the heart, the conscience, the mind, the will, and the emotions. Each plays a vital role in our spiritual life and interaction with God.

The Heart

The heart is central to our spiritual experience. Proverbs 4:23 advises, "Keep your heart with all vigilance, for from it flow the springs of life." The heart, comprising the mind, will, and emotions, is the center of our being and dictates our relationship with God. A pure heart is essential for seeing God and experiencing His presence.

The Conscience

The conscience is the part of our spirit that discerns right from wrong. Hebrews 9:14 highlights its importance: "How much more will the blood of Christ, who through the eternal Spirit offered himself without blemish to God, purify our conscience from dead works to worship the living God!" A clear and active conscience is necessary for maintaining fellowship with God and for spiritual growth.

The Mind

The mind is a component of the heart, responsible for thoughts and understanding. Romans 12:2 emphasizes its transformation: "Do not be conformed to this world, but be transformed by the renewal of your mind, that by testing you may discern what is the will of God, what is good and acceptable and perfect." Renewing our mind aligns it with God's will, enabling us to think and act according to His purposes.

The Will

The will determines our choices and actions. Philippians 2:13 reassures us, "For it is God who works in you, both to will and to work for his good pleasure." A surrendered will allows God's power to operate within us, guiding our decisions and actions towards His divine plan.

The Emotions

Emotions reflect our responses to various situations and stimuli. They play a significant role in our spiritual life. God desires our emotions to be aligned with His, as seen in Romans 12:15, "Rejoice with those who rejoice, weep with those who weep." Healthy emotions foster empathy, compassion, and a deeper connection with God and others.

The Hidden Man of the Heart

1 Peter 3:4 refers to "the hidden person of the heart with the imperishable beauty of a gentle and quiet spirit, which in God's sight is very precious." This hidden man of the heart is our true spiritual self, where God's Spirit dwells and works to transform us into His image. Cultivating this hidden inner self is crucial for spiritual maturity.

The Spirit's Operation in Our Inward Parts

God's Spirit operates within these inward parts, transforming and sanctifying us. Hebrews 4:12 explains, "For the word of God is living and active, sharper than any two-edged sword, piercing to the division of soul and of spirit, of joints and of marrow, and discerning the thoughts and intentions of the heart." The Word of God, through the Spirit, penetrates our innermost being, bringing light and life.

The Practical Application

Practically, we engage our inward parts through prayer, meditation on God's Word, and yielding to the Holy Spirit. This involves a daily practice of turning our hearts to God, maintaining a pure conscience, renewing our mind, surrendering our will, and regulating our emotions. By doing so, we allow the Holy Spirit to fill and transform every aspect of our being.

The inward and hidden parts of our being are integral to experiencing God's economy. By understanding and nurturing these parts, we align ourselves with God's work within us, allowing His Spirit to transform us from the inside out. This transformation is essential for living a life that reflects God's glory and fulfills His divine purpose.

The intersection of economic philosophy and theology reveals a rich tapestry of ethical and moral considerations. Different belief systems offer diverse perspectives on wealth distribution, social justice, and economic behavior, each contributing to the broader discourse on how societies can create fair and just economic systems. As we continue to explore the theology of money, these foundational principles will inform our understanding of contemporary economic practices and their alignment with religious values.

The Function of the Inward and Hidden Parts

In our spiritual journey, understanding the function of our inward and hidden parts is crucial for experiencing the fullness of God's economy. These parts, which include the heart, conscience, mind, will, and emotions, play pivotal roles in our relationship with God and our spiritual growth.

The Heart

The heart, which encompasses the mind, will, and emotions, serves as the central hub of our spiritual life. Proverbs 4:23 advises, "Keep your heart with all vigilance, for from it flow the springs of life." A heart attuned to God is essential for maintaining a vibrant spiritual life and for facilitating the flow of divine life within us.

The Conscience

The conscience, a part of our spirit, acts as an inner moral compass, discerning right from wrong. Hebrews 9:14 emphasizes its importance: "How much more will the blood of Christ, who through the eternal Spirit offered himself without blemish to God, purify our conscience from dead works to worship the living God!" A clear and active conscience is vital for maintaining a close relationship with God and for guiding our moral decisions.

The Mind

The mind, a component of the heart, is responsible for our thoughts and understanding. Romans 12:2 exhorts us to be transformed by the renewing of our mind: "Do not be conformed to this world, but be transformed by the renewal of your mind, that by testing you may discern what is the will of God, what is good and acceptable and perfect." Renewing our mind aligns it with God's will, enabling us to think and act according to His purposes.

The Will

The will determines our choices and actions, shaping our response to God's guidance. Philippians 2:13 reassures us, "For it is God who works in you, both to will and to work for his good pleasure." A surrendered will allows God's power to operate within us, guiding our decisions and actions towards His divine plan.

The Emotions

Emotions reflect our responses to various situations and stimuli and are integral to our spiritual life. God desires our emotions to be aligned with His, fostering empathy, compassion, and a deeper connection with Him and others. Romans 12:15 instructs us to "Rejoice with those who rejoice, weep with those who weep," highlighting the importance of emotional alignment with God's heart.

The Hidden Man of the Heart

1 Peter 3:4 refers to "the hidden person of the heart with the imperishable beauty of a gentle and quiet spirit, which in God's sight is very precious." This hidden man of the heart represents our true spiritual self, where God's Spirit dwells and works to transform us into His image. Cultivating this inner self is essential for spiritual maturity and alignment with God's will.

The Spirit's Operation in Our Inward Parts

God's Spirit operates within these inward parts, transforming and sanctifying us. Hebrews 4:12 explains, "For the word of God is living and active, sharper than any two-edged sword, piercing to the division of soul and of spirit, of joints and of marrow, and discerning the thoughts and intentions of the heart." The Word of God, through the Spirit, penetrates our innermost being, bringing light and life.

Practical Application

Practically engaging our inward parts involves prayer, meditation on God's Word, and yielding to the Holy Spirit. This daily practice of turning our hearts to God, maintaining a pure conscience, renewing our mind, surrendering our will, and regulating our emotions allows the Holy Spirit to fill and transform every aspect of our being.

Conclusion

The function of our inward and hidden parts is integral to experiencing God's economy. By understanding and nurturing these parts, we align ourselves with God's work within us, allowing His Spirit to transform us from the inside out. This transformation is essential for living a life that reflects God's glory and fulfills His divine purpose.

CHAPTER 12

DEALING WITH THE HEART, THE SPIRIT, AND THE SOUL

To fully experience God's economy, we must understand how to deal with our hearts and spirit. These inner parts are crucial for our spiritual growth and our relationship with God.

The Importance of the Heart

The heart, encompassing the mind, will, and emotions, is the control center of our spiritual life. Proverbs 4:23 instructs, "Keep your heart with all vigilance, for from it flow the springs of life." A well-guarded heart ensures that we remain in the flow of divine life, allowing God's essence to permeate our being.

Purifying the Heart

Purifying the heart is essential for a closer walk with God. Matthew 5:8 declares, "Blessed are the pure in heart, for they shall see God." A pure heart is free from mixed motives and distractions, making it receptive to God's presence and guidance. To purify our heart, we must regularly confess our sins, forgive others, and seek God's cleansing.

Aligning the Heart with God's Will

Aligning our heart with God's will involves submitting our desires and intentions to Him. Psalm 37:4 advises, "Delight yourself in the Lord, and he will give you the desires of your heart." When we delight in God, our desires become aligned with His purposes, and He fulfills them in accordance with His will.

The Role of the Spirit

Our spirit is the deepest part of our being, where we commune with God. John 4:24 states, "God is spirit, and those who worship him must worship in spirit and truth."

Engaging our spirit in worship and daily life allows us to connect with God on a profound level, experiencing His presence and guidance.

Strengthening the Spirit

To strengthen our spirit, we must cultivate a life of prayer and meditation on God's Word. Ephesians 3:16-17 says, "That according to the riches of his glory he may grant you to be strengthened with power through his Spirit in your inner being, so that Christ may dwell in your hearts through faith." Strengthening our spirit enables us to withstand spiritual challenges and grow in our relationship with God.

The Spirit's Guidance

The Holy Spirit guides us into all truth and helps us navigate life's complexities. Romans 8:14 affirms, "For all who are led by the Spirit of God are sons of God." Being led by the Spirit involves being sensitive to His promptings and obedient to His direction, ensuring that we walk in God's will.

Practical Steps for Dealing with the Heart and Spirit

Practically, dealing with our heart and spirit involves several steps:

1. Regular Confession and Repentance: Keep your heart pure by confessing sins and repenting regularly.

2. Prayer and Meditation: Strengthen your spirit through consistent prayer and meditation on God's Word.

3. Forgiveness and Reconciliation: Maintain a pure heart by forgiving others and seeking reconciliation.

4. Obedience to the Spirit: Follow the guidance of the Holy Spirit in all areas of life.

Dealing with the heart and spirit is vital for experiencing the fullness of God's economy. By purifying our heart and strengthening our spirit, we align ourselves with God's purposes and allow His life to flow through us. This transformation enables us to live out God's economy, reflecting His glory in our lives.

Dealing with the Soul

To fully engage with God's economy, we must address the soul, which encompasses the mind, will, and emotions.

The soul plays a pivotal role in our spiritual journey and our relationship with God.

Understanding the Soul

The soul, comprising our mind, will, and emotions, is the seat of our personality and individual experiences. Hebrews 4:12 emphasizes the importance of discerning the soul from the spirit: "For the word of God is living and active, sharper than any two-edged sword, piercing to the division of soul and spirit, of joints and of marrow, and discerning the thoughts and intentions of the heart." This discernment is crucial for spiritual growth and alignment with God's purposes.

The Mind

The mind is central to our thoughts, understanding, and reasoning. Romans 12:2 urges us to renew our minds: "Do not be conformed to this world, but be transformed by the renewal of your mind, that by testing you may discern what is the will of God, what is good and acceptable and perfect." Renewing the mind involves aligning our thoughts with God's truth, enabling us to think and act according to His will.

The Will

The will determines our decisions and actions, shaping our response to God's guidance. Philippians 2:13 reassures us, "For it is God who works in you, both to will and to work for his good pleasure." Surrendering our will to God allows His power to operate within us, guiding our choices and actions towards His divine plan.

The Emotions

Emotions reflect our responses to various situations and stimuli and are integral to our spiritual life. God desires our emotions to be aligned with His, fostering empathy, compassion, and a deeper connection with Him and others. Romans 12:15 instructs us to "Rejoice with those who rejoice, weep with those who weep," highlighting the importance of emotional alignment with God's heart.

The Transformation of the Soul

Transformation of the soul is a continuous process involving the renewal of the mind, the alignment of the will, and the regulation of emotions. 2 Corinthians 3:18 explains, "And we all, with unveiled face, beholding the glory of the Lord, are being transformed into the same image from one degree of glory to another; for this comes from the Lord, the Spirit." This transformation aligns our soul with the image of Christ, reshaping our inner being to reflect His glory.

Practical Steps for Dealing with the Soul

Practically engaging our soul involves several steps:

1. Regular Reflection and Confession: Assess your thoughts, decisions, and emotions regularly, confessing and realigning them with God's truth.

2. Prayer and Meditation: Strengthen your soul through consistent prayer and meditation on God's Word, allowing His truth to renew your mind.

3. Surrender and Obedience: Continuously surrender your will to God, seeking His guidance and obeying His directions.

4. Emotional Regulation: Cultivate emotional health by fostering empathy, compassion, and resilience, aligning your emotions with God's heart.

The Digging of Our Inward and Hidden Parts

In our journey to fully experience God's economy, it is essential to delve into our inward and hidden parts—our heart, spirit, mind, will, and emotions. This chapter focuses on the process of examining and dealing with these areas to allow God's life to flow freely within us.

The Heart

The heart is the control center of our being, influencing our thoughts, decisions, and emotions. Proverbs 4:23 highlights its significance: "Keep your heart with all vigilance, for from it flow the springs of life." A heart fully aligned with God is crucial for the proper flow of His life within us.

The Need for Heart Examination

Jeremiah 17:9-10 warns us about the deceitfulness of the heart: "The heart is deceitful above all things, and desperately sick; who can understand it? I the Lord search the heart and test the mind, to give every man according to his ways, according to the fruit of his deeds." Regular examination and purification of our heart are necessary to ensure it remain aligned with God's will.

The Spirit

Our spirit is the deepest part of our being, where we commune with God. John 4:24 states, "God is spirit, and those who worship him must worship in spirit and truth." Engaging our spirit in worship and daily life allows us to connect intimately with God, experiencing His presence and guidance.

Strengthening the Spirit

To strengthen our spirit, we must cultivate a life of prayer and meditation on God's Word. Ephesians 3:16-17 says, "That according to the riches of his glory he may grant you to be strengthened with power through his Spirit in your inner being, so that Christ may dwell in your hearts through faith." Strengthening our spirit enables us to withstand spiritual challenges and grow in our relationship with God.

The Mind

The mind, a critical component of the heart, influences our thoughts and understanding. Romans 12:2 urges us to renew our minds: "Do not be conformed to this world, but be transformed by the renewal of your mind, that by testing you may discern what is the will of God, what is good and acceptable and perfect." Renewing the mind involves aligning our thoughts with God's truth.

The Will

The will determines our decisions and actions. Philippians 2:13 reassures us, "For it is God who works in you, both to will and to work for his good pleasure." A surrendered will allows God's power to operate within us, guiding our choices and actions towards His divine plan.

The Emotions

Emotions are integral to our spiritual life, reflecting our responses to various situations. God desires our emotions to be aligned with His, fostering empathy, compassion, and a deeper connection with Him and others. Romans 12:15 instructs us to "Rejoice with those who rejoice, weep with those who weep," highlighting the importance of emotional alignment with God's heart.

The Process of Digging

The process of digging into our inward and hidden parts involves regular reflection, confession, and submission to God. Hebrews 4:12 explains the importance of this process: "For the word of God is living and active, sharper than any two-edged sword, piercing to the division of soul and of spirit, of joints and of marrow, and discerning the thoughts and intentions of the heart." God's Word, through the Holy Spirit, penetrates our innermost being, revealing areas that need transformation.

Practical Steps for Digging

Practically engaging in this process involves:

1. Self-Examination: Regularly reflect on your thoughts, decisions, and emotions, aligning them with God's truth.

2. Confession and Repentance: Confess sins and seek God's forgiveness, allowing His cleansing power to purify your heart.

3. Prayer and Meditation: Strengthen your spirit through consistent prayer and meditation on God's Word.

4. Surrender and Obedience: Continuously surrender your will to God, seeking His guidance and obeying His directions.

5. Emotional Regulation: Cultivate emotional health by fostering empathy, compassion, and resilience, aligning your emotions with God's heart.

Conclusion

Digging into our inward and hidden parts is essential for experiencing the fullness of God's economy. By examining and dealing with our heart, spirit, mind, will, and emotions, we allow God's Spirit to transform our entire being. This transformation is key to living a life that reflects God's glory and fulfills His divine purpose.

Dealing with the soul is essential for experiencing the fullness of God's economy. By renewing our mind, aligning our will, and regulating our emotions, we allow God's Spirit to transform our entire being. This transformation is key to living a life that reflects God's glory and fulfills His divine purpose.

CHAPTER 13

WEALTH AND VIRTUE

The relationship between material wealth and virtue is a central theme in many religious and philosophical traditions. This chapter explores how various theologies address the connection between wealth and virtues such as generosity, humility, and contentment. It examines the moral and ethical teachings that guide the use and perception of wealth, emphasizing the cultivation of virtues that transcend material possessions.

Generosity

Generosity is universally esteemed across religious traditions as a virtue that transforms wealth into a tool for good.

1. Christianity:

- Biblical Teachings: The Bible emphasizes generosity, encouraging believers to give freely and selflessly. In 2 Corinthians 9:7, Paul writes, "Each of you should give what you have decided in your heart to give, not reluctantly or under compulsion, for God loves a cheerful giver." The story of the Good Samaritan (Luke 10:25-37) exemplifies the virtue of generosity in action.

- Early Church Practices: The early Christian community practiced radical generosity, sharing possessions and resources (Acts 2:44-45). This communal approach to wealth highlighted the importance of supporting one another and addressing the needs of the less fortunate.

Discerning the Spirit from the Soul

In the pursuit of spiritual maturity, one must learn to discern the spirit from the soul. This discernment is essential for understanding God's economy and for experiencing His divine life within us.

The Distinction Between Spirit and Soul

Hebrews 4:12 elucidates the difference: "For the word of God is living and active, sharper than any two-edged sword, piercing to the division of soul and of spirit, of joints and of marrow, and discerning the thoughts and intentions of the heart." The Word of God reveals the distinction between our spirit and soul, enabling us to understand their unique roles in our spiritual life.

The Function of the Spirit

The spirit is the deepest part of our being, where we connect with God. John 4:24 emphasizes this connection: "God is spirit, and those who worship him must worship in spirit and truth." Our spirit is designed for fellowship with God, allowing us to experience His presence and guidance.

The Function of the Soul

The soul, comprising the mind, will, and emotions, is the seat of our personality and individual experiences. It processes our thoughts, decisions, and feelings. While the soul is crucial for daily living, it must be aligned with the spirit to function according to God's purpose.

The Need for Discernment

Discerning the spirit from the soul is vital for spiritual growth. 1 Corinthians 2:14-15 explains, "The natural person does not accept the things of the Spirit of God, for they are folly to him, and he is not able to understand them because they are spiritually discerned. The spiritual person judges all things, but is himself to be judged by no one." Spiritual discernment allows us to differentiate between what is of God and what is of our natural self.

The Process of Discernment

The process of discerning the spirit from the soul involves regular engagement with God's Word, prayer, and the Holy Spirit's guidance. Hebrews 4:12 again highlights the role of God's Word: "For the word of God is living and active... piercing to the division of soul and of spirit." The living Word of God acts as a tool for discerning and dividing the spiritual from the soulish.

Practical Steps for Discernment

Practically, discerning the spirit from the soul involves several steps:

1. Engage with God's Word: Regularly read and meditate on the Bible, allowing it to penetrate and reveal the inner workings of your spirit and soul.

2. Prayer and Reflection: Spend time in prayer, asking the Holy Spirit to illuminate areas where your soul may be overriding your spirit.

3. Spiritual Sensitivity: Cultivate sensitivity to the Holy Spirit's guidance, learning to recognize His promptings versus your own thoughts and emotions.

4. Obedience: Act in obedience to the Spirit's guidance, even when it conflicts with your soulish desires or reasoning.

The Outcome of Proper Discernment

When we correctly discern the spirit from the soul, we align ourselves with God's will and experience a deeper fellowship with Him. This alignment allows us to live according to the Spirit, producing spiritual fruit and fulfilling God's purpose for our lives. Galatians 5:16 encourages us:

"But I say, walk by the Spirit, and you will not gratify the desires of the flesh."

Conclusion

Discerning the spirit from the soul is essential for participating fully in God's economy. By distinguishing these parts and aligning them with God's Word and Spirit, we experience His life and power within us. This discernment is key to living a life that reflects God's glory and fulfills His divine purpose.

2. Islam:

- Zakat and Sadaqah: Generosity is a fundamental principle in Islam, encapsulated in the practices of zakat (obligatory almsgiving) and sadaqah (voluntary charity). Surah Al-Baqarah (2:261) illustrates the value of charity, likening it to a grain that produces multiple ears, each bearing a hundred grains.

- Hadith: The Hadith literature reinforces the importance of generosity. The Prophet Muhammad said, "The believer's shade on the Day of Resurrection will be his charity" (Al-Tirmidhi).

3. Buddhism:

- Dana (Giving): Generosity, or dana, is a foundational virtue in Buddhism. It is considered the first of the Ten Perfections (Paramitas) and is essential for spiritual development. Acts of giving, whether material or immaterial, help cultivate a spirit of detachment and compassion.

- Sutta Teachings: The Pali Canon contains numerous teachings on the importance of generosity. The Digha Nikaya, for instance, describes how acts of giving lead to spiritual benefits and create positive karma.

Humility

Humility, or the recognition of one's limitations and the avoidance of arrogance, is another virtue deeply connected to wealth.

1. Christianity:

- Teachings of Jesus: Jesus frequently taught about the dangers of pride and the value of humility. In Matthew 23:12, He states, "For those who exalt themselves will be humbled, and those who humble themselves will be exalted."

- Parables: The parable of the Pharisee and the Tax Collector (Luke 18:9-14) contrasts the humility of the tax collector with the pride of the Pharisee, illustrating the virtue of humility in the eyes of God.

2. Islam:

- Quranic Guidance: The Quran emphasizes humility, particularly in the context of wealth. Surah Al-Furqan (25:63) describes the "servants of the Most Merciful" as those who "walk on the earth humbly."

- Prophetic Example: The Prophet Muhammad is renowned for his humility, despite his significant influence and leadership. His life serves as a model for Muslims to follow, demonstrating how humility should accompany wealth and power.

3. Hinduism:

- Bhagavad Gita: The Bhagavad Gita extols the virtue of humility as a key attribute of a wise person. In Chapter 13, Verse 8, humility (amanitvam) is listed as one of the qualities that lead to true knowledge.

- Philosophical Teachings: Hindu philosophy teaches that true humility involves recognizing the divine presence in all beings and understanding the transient nature of material wealth.

Contentment

Contentment, or satisfaction with what one has, is a virtue that counters the insatiable desire for more wealth.

1. Christianity:

- Paul's Teachings: The Apostle Paul speaks about contentment in Philippians 4:11-12, stating, "I have learned to be content whatever the circumstances." This teaching emphasizes finding satisfaction in God's provision, regardless of material wealth.

- Proverbs: The book of Proverbs also highlights the value of contentment, with Proverbs 30:8-9 expressing a desire for neither poverty nor riches, but rather for daily bread.

2. Islam:

- Rida (Contentment): In Islam, contentment (rida) is seen as a state of satisfaction with God's will and provision. Surah Ash-Shura (42:36) encourages believers to find contentment in what Allah has provided, as worldly possessions are fleeting.

- Hadith: The Prophet Muhammad said, "Riches are not from an abundance of worldly goods, but from a contented mind" (Sahih Bukhari), underscoring the spiritual nature of true wealth.

3. Buddhism:

- Simplicity and Moderation: Buddhism teaches the value of simplicity and moderation, encouraging contentment with minimal possessions. The principle of Right Livelihood in the Noble Eightfold Path advocates for a life that is not driven by excessive desire for material wealth.

- Meditation Practices: Buddhist meditation practices help cultivate a sense of inner peace and contentment, reducing attachment to material possessions and fostering a deeper appreciation for the present moment.

Conclusion

The theological perspectives on wealth and virtue highlight the importance of using material resources in ways that promote ethical and spiritual growth. Generosity, humility, and contentment are virtues that transcend material wealth, guiding individuals toward a more balanced and fulfilling life. As we continue to explore the theology of money, these virtues will serve as essential touchstones for understanding how wealth can be aligned with spiritual and moral values.

CHAPTER 14

CAPITALISM, SOCIALISM, AND THEOLOGICAL PERSPECTIVES

Economic systems such as capitalism and socialism present differing approaches to managing resources, wealth distribution, and societal welfare. These systems often intersect with theological doctrines, creating areas of both compatibility and conflict. This chapter analyzes how theological principles align or clash with the core tenets of capitalism and socialism, exploring the implications for social justice and ethical behavior.

Capitalism and Theology

Capitalism, characterized by private ownership, free markets, and the profit motive, has been both supported and criticized from theological standpoints.

1. Compatibility with Theological Doctrines:

- Individual Responsibility and Freedom: Many theological perspectives value individual responsibility and freedom, principles that are central to capitalism. The Protestant work ethic, as described by Max Weber, aligns with capitalist ideals by emphasizing hard work, frugality, and economic success as signs of divine favor.

- Stewardship: Capitalism's focus on personal property can align with the concept of stewardship found in many religious traditions. For instance, the Bible teaches that individuals are stewards of their resources and should use them responsibly for the glory of God and the betterment of society (1 Peter 4:10).

2. Conflicts with Theological Doctrines:

- Wealth Inequality: One of the major theological critiques of capitalism is its tendency to create significant wealth inequality. The Bible, Quran, and other religious texts emphasize the importance of social justice and caring for the poor, which can be at odds with the capitalist accumulation of wealth.

- Materialism: Capitalism's emphasis on consumerism and material success can conflict with spiritual teachings that prioritize inner values over external wealth. Jesus' warning in Matthew 6:24 against serving both God and money highlights this tension.

Socialism and Theology

Socialism, with its focus on collective ownership and equitable distribution of resources, also intersects with theological principles in various ways.

1. Compatibility with Theological Doctrines:
- Equality and Social Justice: Theological teachings that emphasize equality and social justice often align well with socialist principles. For example, the early Christian community described in Acts 2:44-45 practiced a form of communal living, sharing all possessions to ensure that no one was in need.

- Support for the Poor: Socialism's aim to reduce poverty and provide for the basic needs of all citizens resonates with religious imperatives to care for the marginalized and the vulnerable. Islamic principles of zakat and sadaqah, and Jewish concepts of tzedakah, reflect this alignment.

2. Conflicts with Theological Doctrines:

- Individual Freedom: Critics argue that socialism can infringe on individual freedoms by placing too much control in the hands of the state. This can be seen as conflicting with the theological value of free will and personal responsibility.

- Secularism: Some forms of socialism promote secularism and can be perceived as opposing religious institutions and practices. This potential conflict is particularly evident in contexts where socialist regimes have sought to limit the influence of religion.

Christianity and Economic Systems

Christianity presents diverse views on capitalism and socialism, reflecting its broad theological spectrum.

1. Capitalism:

- Support: Some Christian denominations and theologians support capitalism for its promotion of individual initiative, entrepreneurship, and the potential to create wealth that can be used for charitable purposes.

- Criticism: Others criticize capitalism for fostering greed, exploitation, and inequality. Liberation theology, particularly influential in Latin America, calls for a preferential option for the poor and critiques capitalist structures that perpetuate poverty and injustice.

2. Socialism:

- Support: Christian socialists advocate for economic systems that reflect the communal sharing and social justice principles found in early Christian communities. They argue that socialism's emphasis on equitable distribution of resources aligns with biblical teachings on justice and compassion.

- Criticism: Some Christians oppose socialism, viewing it as restrictive of personal freedom and incompatible with individual stewardship of resources. They also express concerns about socialism's potential to marginalize religious practices in favor of state control.

Islam and Economic Systems

Islamic economic principles offer a unique perspective on capitalism and socialism, blending elements of both systems.

1. Capitalism:

- Support: Islam supports free enterprise and trade, as long as they are conducted ethically and justly. The Quran and Hadith encourage fair business practices, honest trade, and the prohibition of exploitative practices such as riba (usury).

- Criticism: Islamic teachings criticize unrestrained capitalism for fostering greed and inequality. The emphasis on zakat and wealth redistribution reflects a concern for ensuring that the poor and needy are cared for.

2. Socialism:

- Support: Islamic principles of social justice, charity, and the communal welfare align with socialist ideals. The concept of waqf (endowment) is similar to socialist ideas of public welfare.

- Criticism: Islam emphasizes private property and individual responsibility, which can conflict with socialist ideals of collective ownership. Additionally, Islam's focus on faith and spirituality may be at odds with secular socialist regimes.

Hinduism, Buddhism, and Economic Systems

Hindu and Buddhist teachings also interact with capitalist and socialist principles, though in distinct ways.

1. Hinduism:

- Capitalism: Hinduism's concept of artha (pursuit of wealth) acknowledges the importance of economic activity, provided it is pursued ethically within the framework of dharma (moral duty).

- Socialism: The communal aspects of Hindu society, such as the joint family system, reflect socialist principles of shared resources. However, the caste system's historical rigidity can conflict with socialist ideals of equality.

2. Buddhism:

- Capitalism: Buddhism's emphasis on right livelihood and ethical conduct supports fair and honest economic practices, which can align with regulated capitalist systems.

- Socialism: Buddhist teachings on compassion, non-attachment, and the alleviation of suffering align well with socialist principles of social welfare and equality.

Conclusion

The interplay between economic systems and theological principles reveals a complex and nuanced landscape. While capitalism and socialism each offer elements that resonate with various theological doctrines, they also present challenges and conflicts. By examining these intersections, we gain a deeper understanding of how economic practices can be aligned with spiritual and moral values, striving for systems that promote both economic efficiency and social justice.

CHAPTER 15

THE PROSPERITY GOSPEL

The prosperity gospel, also known as the "health and wealth gospel" or "faith theology," is a controversial religious belief that emphasizes material wealth and physical well-being as evidence of God's favor. This chapter explores the theological foundations of the prosperity gospel, its key proponents, and the impact it has on religious communities, both positive and negative.

Theological Foundations of the Prosperity Gospel

The prosperity gospel is rooted in specific interpretations of Christian scripture and theology. Its primary tenets include:

1. Biblical Promises of Blessing:
- Old Testament: Advocates of the prosperity gospel often cite Old Testament passages that promise blessings for obedience. For example, Deuteronomy 28:1-14 outlines blessings for those who follow God's commandments, including prosperity, health, and success.

- New Testament: New Testament scriptures are also used to support prosperity teachings. John 10:10, where Jesus says, "I have come that they may have life, and have it to the full," is interpreted as a promise of abundant life, including material wealth.

2. Faith and Positive Confession:
- Word of Faith Movement: The prosperity gospel is closely associated with the Word of Faith movement, which emphasizes the power of spoken words and positive confession. Followers believe that verbal declarations can bring about physical and financial blessings, based on scriptures like Mark 11:24, "Therefore I tell you, whatever you

ask for in prayer, believe that you have received it, and it will be yours."

- Seed-Faith Principle: This principle teaches that giving money to the church or ministries, often referred to as "sowing a seed," will result in financial blessings from God. This idea is drawn from passages like Luke 6:38, "Give, and it will be given to you."

Key Proponents of the Prosperity Gospel

Several high-profile preachers and televangelists have popularized the prosperity gospel, including:

1. Oral Roberts:

- Early Influence: Oral Roberts is often credited with pioneering the prosperity gospel in the mid-20th century. He introduced the concept of seed-faith giving and emphasized God's desire for believers to be healthy and prosperous.

- Legacy: Roberts' teachings laid the groundwork for future prosperity preachers and influenced a generation of televangelists.

2. Kenneth Hagin:

- Word of Faith Movement: Kenneth Hagin, known as the father of the Word of Faith movement, taught extensively on the power of faith and positive confession. His books and sermons have been instrumental in spreading prosperity theology.

3. Joel Osteen:

- Popular Appeal: Joel Osteen is one of the most well-known proponents of the prosperity gospel today. His books and sermons, which focus on positive thinking and God's desire to bless believers, have attracted a large following.

Impact on Religious Communities

The prosperity gospel has had significant and varied impacts on religious communities:

1. Positive Impact:

- Encouragement and Hope: For many believers, the prosperity gospel provides a message of hope and encouragement, particularly in difficult economic circumstances. The emphasis on positive thinking and faith can lead to increased motivation and personal growth.

- Generosity: The principle of seed-faith giving encourages generosity and financial support for churches and ministries, which can result in expanded charitable activities and community support.

2. Negative Impact:

- Financial Exploitation: Critics argue that the prosperity gospel can lead to financial exploitation, with believers giving beyond their means in the hope of receiving blessings. This has led to accusations of manipulation and profiteering among some preachers.

- Spiritual Disillusionment: When promised financial and health miracles do not materialize, some believers experience spiritual disillusionment and loss of faith. This can be particularly damaging for vulnerable individuals who have invested heavily in these teachings.

- Theological Criticisms: Many theologians and religious leaders criticize the prosperity gospel for promoting a materialistic and transactional view of God. They argue that it distorts core Christian teachings about suffering, self-sacrifice, and the nature of true blessing.

Criticism and Controversy

The prosperity gospel has faced significant criticism from within and outside religious circles:

1. Theological Concerns:

- Distortion of the Gospel: Critics argue that the prosperity gospel distorts the Christian message by placing excessive emphasis on material wealth and physical health, rather than spiritual growth and eternal salvation.

- Ignoring Suffering: The prosperity gospel's focus on positive outcomes can lead to a lack of understanding and compassion for those who suffer. It can imply that suffering is a result of insufficient faith, which contradicts many biblical teachings about the role of suffering in spiritual development.

2. Ethical Issues:

- Exploitation: There are ethical concerns about the ways some prosperity gospel preachers raise funds, often pressuring followers to give large donations with promises of divine rewards. This has led to numerous scandals and legal issues.

- Inequality: The wealth accumulated by some prosperity gospel preachers stands in stark contrast to the financial struggles of many of their followers, raising questions about the ethical implications of such disparities.

The Riches of Resurrection

Understanding and experiencing the riches of resurrection is vital to living a victorious Christian life. The resurrection of Jesus Christ is the cornerstone of our faith and the source of our new life in Him.

The Covenant of Resurrection

Hebrews 8:10-11 declares, "For this is the covenant that I will make with the house of Israel after those days, says the Lord: I will put my laws into their minds, and write them on their hearts, and I will be their God, and they shall be my people. And they shall not teach everyone his fellow citizen, and everyone his brother, saying, 'Know the Lord,' for all shall know me, from the least to the greatest of them." This new covenant signifies the inward working of God's law and His anointing within us, made possible through the resurrection of Christ.

The Anointing Within

1 John 2:27 explains, "And as for you, the anointing which you received from Him abides in you, and you have no need for anyone to teach you; but as His anointing teaches you about all things, and is true and is not a lie, and just as it has taught you, you abide in Him." This anointing, a result of the resurrection, teaches us and guides us in all truth, emphasizing our direct relationship with God through the Holy Spirit.

The Inner Law and Anointing

The inner law and the anointing within us are aspects of the resurrection life. The inner law refers to God's commandments written on our hearts, guiding us from within. The anointing is the Holy Spirit's work in us, teaching and leading us in our daily walk with God. These elements eliminate the need for external guidance, as we have the living presence of God within us.

The Cross and Resurrection

The cross and resurrection are inseparable in the Christian experience. Romans 6:4 states, "We were buried therefore with Him by baptism into death, in order that, just as Christ was raised from the dead by the glory of the Father, we too might walk in newness of life." The cross puts to death our old self, and the resurrection brings forth a new life in Christ, enabling us to live according to God's will.

The Power of Resurrection

Philippians 3:10-11 highlights the desire to know the power of Christ's resurrection: "That I may know Him and the power of His resurrection, and may share His sufferings, becoming like Him in His death, that by any means possible I may attain the resurrection from the dead." The power of resurrection is not only a future hope but a present reality that empowers us to overcome sin and live victoriously.

Practical Steps to Experience Resurrection Life

1. Embrace the Cross: Daily take up your cross, denying self and following Christ's example.

2. Depend on the Holy Spirit: Rely on the Holy Spirit's anointing to teach and guide you in all aspects of life.

3. Seek Daily Renewal: Engage in regular prayer and meditation on God's Word to renew your mind and spirit.

4. Live by Faith: Trust in the power of Christ's resurrection to enable you to live a life that pleases God.

The Outcome of Resurrection Life

Living by the riches of resurrection results in a transformed life that reflects God's glory. Colossians 3:1-3 encourages us, "If then you have been raised with Christ, seek the things that are above, where Christ is, seated at the right hand of God. Set your minds on things that are above, not on things that are on earth. For you have died, and your life is hidden with Christ in God." This heavenly perspective shapes our actions, priorities, and values, aligning them with God's eternal purposes.

Conclusion

The riches of resurrection are central to experiencing the fullness of God's economy. By understanding and embracing this principle, we live in the power of Christ's resurrection, reflecting His life in our daily walk. This transformation is key to fulfilling God's purpose and manifesting His glory through us.

Conclusion

The prosperity gospel remains a highly controversial and influential movement within contemporary Christianity. While it offers a message of hope and empowerment to many, it also raises significant theological, ethical, and practical concerns. As we continue to explore the theology of money, understanding the complexities of the prosperity gospel provides valuable insights into the broader discourse on wealth, faith, and the ethical use of resources in religious communities.

CHAPTER 16

POVERTY AND THEODICY

The existence of poverty and suffering in a world governed by a benevolent deity is a profound theological dilemma known as theodicy. This chapter explores various theological explanations for poverty and suffering across different religious traditions, examining how they reconcile these realities with the belief in a loving and just God.

Christian Perspectives on Poverty and Theodicy

Christianity offers multiple explanations for the presence of poverty and suffering, each rooted in scripture and theological tradition.

1. Original Sin and Human Free Will:

- The Fall: The Christian doctrine of original sin, stemming from Adam and Eve's disobedience in the Garden of Eden (Genesis 3), explains the presence of suffering and evil as a consequence of humanity's fall from grace. This event introduced sin and suffering into the world, impacting all aspects of human life, including economic conditions.

- Human Agency: The exercise of free will can lead to unjust systems and structures that perpetuate poverty. Christianity teaches that while God allows free will, humans are responsible for the choices that result in social injustices and economic disparities.

2. Testing and Character Building:

- Divine Purpose: Some theological interpretations suggest that suffering and poverty serve a divine purpose, testing faith and building character. The story of Job exemplifies this view, where Job's suffering is seen as a test of his righteousness and fidelity to God (Job 1-2).

- Spiritual Growth: Suffering can lead to spiritual growth and greater reliance on God. The Apostle Paul speaks of rejoicing in suffering because it produces perseverance, character, and hope (Romans 5:3-5).

3. Redemptive Suffering:

- Participation in Christ's Suffering: Christian theology often views suffering as a way to participate in the suffering of Christ. Paul describes his own hardships as sharing in the sufferings of Christ (Philippians 3:10).

- Redemption through Suffering: The belief that Christ's suffering and sacrifice have redemptive value extends to human suffering, suggesting that enduring poverty and hardship can have spiritual significance and lead to deeper faith.

Islamic Perspectives on Poverty and Theodicy

Islam addresses poverty and suffering through its theological and ethical framework, offering insights into their purpose and the believer's response.

1. Divine Wisdom and Tests:

- Purposeful Trials: The Quran teaches that poverty and suffering are tests from Allah to assess faith and patience. Surah Al-Baqarah (2:155) states, "We will surely test you with something of fear and hunger and a loss of wealth and lives and fruits, but give good tidings to the patient."

- Divine Wisdom: Suffering is part of Allah's greater plan, which may be beyond human understanding. Believers are encouraged to trust in Allah's wisdom and maintain faith through adversity.

2. Zakat and Social Responsibility:

- Obligatory Charity: The institution of zakat (almsgiving) is central to Islamic teachings on poverty. It serves as a means to redistribute wealth and alleviate poverty, ensuring that the needs of the poor are met (Surah At-Tawbah 9:60).

- Community Support: Islam emphasizes the responsibility of the community to care for its members. The Prophet Muhammad said, "He is not a believer whose stomach is filled while his neighbor goes hungry" (Hadith).

3. Contentment and Gratitude:

- Inner Peace: Islam teaches that true wealth lies in contentment and gratitude, rather than material possessions. The Quran encourages believers to be grateful for what they have and to find peace in their relationship with Allah (Surah Ibrahim 14:7).

Hindu Perspectives on Poverty and Theodicy

Hinduism offers diverse explanations for poverty and suffering, rooted in its complex theological and philosophical traditions.

1. Karma and Reincarnation:

- Law of Karma: Hinduism explains suffering through the law of karma, where one's actions in past lives affect their present circumstances. Poverty can be seen as a result of past actions, serving as a means for the soul's growth and purification.

- Cycle of Rebirth: The cycle of samsara (rebirth) provides a framework for understanding suffering. Each life is an opportunity to improve one's karma and progress toward liberation (moksha).

2. Dharma and Duty:

- Righteous Living: Hindu teachings emphasize living according to one's dharma (duty) to create a harmonious society. Fulfilling one's responsibilities and acting ethically are seen as ways to mitigate suffering and contribute to social well-being.

- Charity and Compassion: Acts of charity (dana) are encouraged to help those in need and to reduce suffering. The

Bhagavad Gita highlights the importance of selfless service and helping others.

Buddhist Perspectives on Poverty and Theodicy

Buddhism addresses suffering (dukkha) as a fundamental aspect of existence, offering insights into its causes and ways to overcome it.

1. The Four Noble Truths:
   - Nature of Suffering: The First Noble Truth acknowledges that suffering is an inherent part of life. The Second Noble Truth identifies desire and attachment as the primary causes of suffering.
   - Path to Liberation: The Third and Fourth Noble Truths provide a path to overcoming suffering through the Eightfold Path, which includes ethical conduct, mental discipline, and wisdom.

2. Compassion and Altruism:
   - Bodhisattva Ideal: In Mahayana Buddhism, the bodhisattva ideal emphasizes compassion and the commitment to alleviate the suffering of all beings. This includes addressing poverty and social injustice.

- Charitable Acts: Generosity (dana) is a key virtue in Buddhism, encouraging acts of kindness and support for those in need as part of one's spiritual practice.

Jewish Perspectives on Poverty and Theodicy

Judaism offers insights into the existence of poverty and suffering through its ethical teachings and covenantal relationship with God.

1. Covenantal Relationship:
- Divine Justice: The Hebrew Bible often portrays suffering as a consequence of collective disobedience to God's commandments. The covenantal relationship between God and Israel includes both blessings for obedience and curses for disobedience (Deuteronomy 28).
- Prophetic Calls for Justice: The prophets frequently call for social justice and care for the poor, emphasizing that true worship includes ethical treatment of the marginalized (Isaiah 58:6-7).

2. Human Responsibility:
- Tikkun Olam: The concept of tikkun olam (repairing the world) reflects the Jewish commitment to social

justice and alleviating suffering. This includes efforts to address poverty and create a more just society.

- Charity and Justice: Tzedakah (charity) is a central tenet of Judaism, seen as both a moral obligation and a means to achieve social justice. Leviticus 19:9-10 instructs the community to leave portions of their harvest for the poor and the stranger.

Conclusion

God's eternal plan, His economy, is unveiled throughout the sixty-six books of the Scriptures. At the very beginning, God is depicted creating man as the focal point of all creation, with the purpose of expressing Himself. In His divine economy, God intended for man to be the center of His entire universe, expressing His divine essence.

Man Between Two Trees

In the beginning, we encounter two significant trees in the Word of God: the tree of life and the tree of the knowledge of good and evil (Genesis 2). To grasp God's plan, we must thoroughly understand the significance of these two trees. After creating man, God placed him before these trees, with man's life and destiny hinging on his interaction with them. God instructed man to be cautious about partaking of these trees. The outcome of man's life—life or death—depended entirely on how he dealt with these trees. Eating from the tree of the knowledge of good and evil would result in death, while partaking of the tree of life would lead to life.

The Tree of Life

The tree of life symbolizes God as the source of life. John 15:5 parallels this concept: "I am the vine; you are the branches. Whoever abides in me and I in him, he it is that bears much fruit, for apart from me you can do nothing." The tree of life represents a life dependent on God, drawing sustenance from Him, and manifesting divine life.

The Tree of Knowledge of Good and Evil

Conversely, the tree of the knowledge of good and evil represents independence from God. It signifies a life based on self-reliance, knowledge, and human effort, devoid of divine life. Genesis 3:6 narrates the consequences of partaking from this tree: "So when the woman saw that the tree was good for food and that it was a delight to the eyes, and that the tree was to be desired to make one wise, she took of its fruit and ate, and she also gave some to her husband who was with her, and he ate." This act led to spiritual death and separation from God.

The Significance of the Trees

The two trees represent two distinct principles of living: living by God's life versus living by human knowledge and effort. God's instruction to man was clear: eating from the tree of life would result in life, while eating from the tree of knowledge would lead to death. This dichotomy underscores the importance of choosing to live by God's life and not by self-reliance.

The New Testament Fulfillment

In the New Testament, Jesus Christ embodies the tree of life. John 6:57 states, "As the living Father sent me, and I live because of the Father, so whoever feeds on me, he also will live because of me." Jesus is the source of divine life, and abiding in Him ensures eternal life. The New Testament calls believers to partake of Christ, the true vine, and reject the principle of living by self-effort, represented by the Tree of Knowledge.

Conclusion

The account of the two trees in Genesis is foundational to understanding God's economy. It illustrates the choice between living by divine life or by human knowledge. God's eternal plan is for man to express Him by partaking of His life. By choosing the tree of life, we align ourselves with God's purpose, living in dependence on Him and expressing His divine essence.

CHAPTER 17

CONSUMERISM AND SPIRITUAL FULFILLMENT

Consumerism, characterized by the relentless pursuit of material goods and services, dominates modern society. This chapter examines the theological implications of consumer culture, exploring whether materialism aligns with or contradicts spiritual values. We will consider perspectives from various religious traditions to understand how consumerism impacts spiritual fulfillment and ethical living.

Consumerism in Contemporary Society

1. Definition and Characteristics:
    - Material Acquisition: Consumerism emphasizes acquiring and accumulating material goods as a primary means of achieving happiness and status.

- Economic Growth: It drives economic growth through increased production and consumption, often at the expense of environmental and social well-being.

- Cultural Norms: Consumer culture shapes societal norms and values, influencing how individuals define success and self-worth.

2. Consequences:

- Environmental Impact: Overconsumption leads to resource depletion, pollution, and environmental degradation.

- Social Inequality: Consumerism can exacerbate social inequalities, as access to material goods often reflects and reinforces economic disparities.

- Psychological Effects: The pursuit of material wealth can lead to stress, dissatisfaction, and a perpetual sense of inadequacy.

Theological Perspectives on Consumerism

Christianity:

1. Biblical Teachings:

- Warnings Against Materialism: Jesus warns against the dangers of materialism, stating in Matthew 6:24, "You cannot serve both God and money." The parable of the rich fool (Luke 12:16-21) underscores the futility of accumulating wealth without spiritual richness.

- Simplicity and Generosity: Christian teachings advocate for simplicity and generosity. In 1 Timothy 6:10, Paul writes, "For the love of money is a root of all kinds of evil," encouraging believers to find contentment in godliness rather than material wealth.

2. Spiritual Fulfillment:

- Inner Transformation: Christianity emphasizes spiritual fulfillment through a relationship with God, personal transformation, and service to others. The Beatitudes (Matthew 5:3-12) highlight virtues such as humility, mercy, and peacemaking as pathways to true happiness.

- Community and Compassion: The early Christian community practiced communal living and sharing of resources (Acts 2:44-45), reflecting a countercultural approach to wealth and consumption.

The Fellowship of Life

1 John 1:3 declares, "That which we have seen and heard we proclaim also to you, so that you too may have

fellowship with us; and indeed, our fellowship is with the Father and with his Son Jesus Christ." This fellowship is a shared participation in the divine life of God, fostering a deep and abiding relationship with Him.

The Role of the Holy Spirit

The Holy Spirit is the agent of this fellowship. 2 Corinthians 13:14 emphasizes, "The grace of the Lord Jesus Christ and the love of God and the fellowship of the Holy Spirit be with you all." Through the Spirit, we experience the grace and love of God, enabling us to commune with Him continually.

The Sense of Life

The sense of life refers to the inner consciousness of God's presence and guidance. Romans 8:6 explains, "For to set the mind on the flesh is death, but to set the mind on the Spirit is life and peace." This sense of life helps us discern the leading of the Holy Spirit and aligns our thoughts and actions with God's will.

The Operation of the Inner Sense

The inner sense of life operates through the indwelling Spirit, who convicts, guides, and comforts us. John 16:13 states, "When the Spirit of truth comes, he will guide you into all the truth, for he will not speak on his authority, but whatever he hears he will speak, and he will declare to you the things that are to come." This guidance ensures that we remain in tune with God's purposes.

Practical Steps to Enhance Fellowship

1. Prayer and Meditation: Regular prayer and meditation on God's Word deepen our fellowship with Him.

2. Obedience to the Spirit: Responding promptly to the Holy Spirit's leading strengthens our inner sense of life.

3. Confession and Repentance: Maintaining a clear conscience through confession and repentance keeps our fellowship with God unbroken.

4. Engagement with the Community: Participating in the body of Christ enhances our fellowship, as we share and grow together in faith.

The Outcome of Enhanced Fellowship

Living in the fellowship of life and with a heightened sense of life results in a transformed and victorious Christian life. Galatians 5:22-23 lists the fruit of the Spirit, which are evident in a life deeply connected with God: "But the fruit of the Spirit is love, joy, peace, patience, kindness, goodness, faithfulness, gentleness, self-control; against such things there is no law." These attributes reflect the character of Christ and the impact of the Holy Spirit's work within us.

The fellowship of life and the sense of life are crucial for experiencing the fullness of God's economy. By nurturing our relationship with God through the Holy Spirit, we align our lives with His will and manifest His divine life in our daily walk. This intimate fellowship and inner sense of life are essential for living out God's purpose and glorifying Him in all that we do.

The Exercise of and Entrance into the Spirit

In our spiritual journey, the exercise of our spirit and the entrance into it are crucial for experiencing the fullness of God's economy. This chapter explores the importance of actively engaging our spirit and provides practical steps for entering into this deeper spiritual reality.

The Need for Exercising the Spirit

Exercising our spirit is essential for maintaining a vibrant and dynamic relationship with God. 1 Timothy 4:7-8 instructs us, "Train yourself for godliness; for while bodily training is of some value, godliness is of value in every way, as it holds promise for the present life and also for the life to come." Spiritual exercise involves actively engaging our spirit in prayer, worship, and fellowship with God.

The Role of the Holy Spirit

The Holy Spirit plays a vital role in helping us exercise our spirit. Romans 8:26 says, "Likewise the Spirit helps us in our weakness. For we do not know what to pray for as we ought, but the Spirit himself intercedes for us with groanings too deep for words." The Holy Spirit empowers and guides us in our spiritual exercises, ensuring that our efforts align with God's will.

Practical Steps for Exercising the Spirit

1. Daily Prayer: Regular, heartfelt prayer is a fundamental way to exercise the spirit. Philippians 4:6 encourages us, "Do not be anxious about anything, but in everything by prayer and supplication with thanksgiving let your requests be made known to God."

2. Meditation on Scripture: Reflecting on God's Word nourishes our spirit. Psalm 1:2 highlights the importance of meditation: "But his delight is in the law of the Lord, and on his law, he meditates day and night."

3. Worship and Praise: Engaging in worship and praise brings us into God's presence. Psalm 100:4 invites us, "Enter his gates with thanksgiving, and his courts with praise! Give thanks to him; bless his name!"

4. Fellowship with Believers: Regular fellowship with other believers strengthens our spirit. Hebrews 10:24-25 reminds us, "And let us consider how to stir up one another to love and good works, not neglecting to meet together, as is the habit of some, but encouraging one another, and all the more as you see the Day drawing near."

The Entrance into the Spirit

Entering into the spirit involves a conscious decision to live by the Spirit rather than by the flesh. Galatians 5:16

instructs, "But I say, walk by the Spirit, and you will not gratify the desires of the flesh." This entrance is a daily commitment to follow the Holy Spirit's leading in every aspect of our lives.

The Benefits of Living in the Spirit

Living in the spirit yields numerous benefits, including peace, joy, and a deeper understanding of God's will. Romans 8:6 explains, "For to set the mind on the flesh is death, but to set the mind on the Spirit is life and peace." The Holy Spirit brings life and peace to our souls, guiding us in our walk with God.

The exercise of and entrance into the spirit are essential for experiencing the fullness of God's economy. By actively engaging our spirit through prayer, meditation, worship, and fellowship, we align ourselves with God's purposes and allow His life to flow through us. This dynamic spiritual life enables us to live according to God's will and reflect His glory in all we do.

The Indwelling Christ

Galatians 2:20 states, "I have been crucified with Christ. It is no longer I who live, but Christ who lives in me. And the life I now live in the flesh I live by faith in the Son of God, who loved me and gave himself for me." This verse highlights the profound truth that Christ lives within us. His presence in our spirit transforms our entire being and empowers us to live according to God's will.

The Mystery of Christ in Us

Colossians 1:27 reveals the mystery of Christ's indwelling: "To them God chose to make known how great among the Gentiles are the riches of the glory of this mystery, which is Christ in you, the hope of glory." This mystery, once hidden, is now made known to believers. Christ's presence in us is the hope of glory, the assurance of our ultimate transformation and glorification.

The Spirit of Christ

Romans 8:9 emphasizes the role of the Spirit of Christ: "You, however, are not in the flesh but in the Spirit, if in fact the Spirit of God dwells in you. Anyone who does not have the Spirit of Christ does not belong to him." The Spirit of

Christ indwells every believer, guiding, empowering, and transforming us from within. This indwelling Spirit is the source of our spiritual life and growth.

The Practical Experience of Christ in Us

1. Daily Fellowship: Engage in regular fellowship with Christ through prayer and meditation on His Word. This daily communion strengthens our relationship with Him and deepens our awareness of His presence.

2. Obedience to the Spirit: Follow the promptings of the Holy Spirit, allowing Him to guide your thoughts, decisions, and actions. Romans 8:14 affirms, "For all who are led by the Spirit of God are sons of God."

3. Manifesting Christ's Life: Let Christ's life be evident in your behavior, reflecting His character and love to those around you. Galatians 5:22-23 describes the fruit of the Spirit, which are the visible attributes of a life led by Christ.

The Benefits of Recognizing Christ in Us

Recognizing and living by the reality of Christ in us brings numerous benefits:

1. Assurance of Salvation: Knowing that Christ dwells in us provides the assurance of our salvation and eternal security.

2. Spiritual Empowerment: The indwelling Christ empowers us to overcome sin and live victoriously.

3. Inner Peace: Christ's presence brings peace that surpasses all understanding, even in the midst of trials.

4. Transformation: The continual presence of Christ transforms us into His image, as stated in 2 Corinthians 3:18, "And we all, with unveiled face, beholding the glory of the Lord, are being transformed into the same image from one degree of glory to another."

The hidden Christ in our spirit is the foundation of the Christian life. By recognizing and living according to this profound truth, we experience the fullness of God's economy. Christ's indwelling presence empowers us to live a life that reflects His glory and fulfills His divine purpose. Embrace this reality, and let Christ's life shine through you, transforming you from the inside out.

The Tripartite Nature of Man

Before God could fulfill His intention, Satan, the enemy of God, infiltrated the body of man. Consequently, in the members of our body, there is sin—sin personified. As an unlawful ruler, it can dominate and compel us to act against our will. Satan, as the evil nature and the law of sin, resides in us to corrupt our body. The flesh, therefore, is the body tainted by Satan, and in it, no good thing dwells (Romans 7:18). Our flesh serves the law of sin, opposing both our mind and our will (Romans 7:15, 20).

The Invasion and Indwelling

Satan came into our body as the law of sin, but when we were saved, the Triune God came to dwell in our spirit as our life. Christ, as our life, resides in our spirit. Thus, in our soul, we have the self. We are complex beings with three significant presences within us: Adam, representing humanity; Satan, representing sin; and the Lord, representing divine life. This makes us a battleground where Satan and God contend. Satan takes our body as his base, while God takes our spirit as His stronghold.

The Church as the Body of Christ

The Church, as the Body of Christ, plays a crucial role in God's economy. Ephesians 1:22-23 states, "And he put all things under his feet and gave him as head over all things to the church, which is his body, the fullness of him who fills all in all." The Church is the collective expression of Christ, filled with His presence and life. As believers, we are called to live out this reality, allowing Christ to be manifested through us individually and corporately.

The Process of Dispensation

God's dispensation involves the Father being embodied in the Son, and the Son being realized in the Spirit. This divine process allows God's essence to be imparted into us. The Triune God—the Father, the Son, and the Holy Spirit—work together to dispense the fullness of God into humanity. This process is described in 2 Corinthians 13:14, "The grace of the Lord Jesus Christ and the love of God and the fellowship of the Holy Spirit be with you all." Here, we see the grace of the Son, the love of the Father, and the fellowship of the Holy Spirit working together to accomplish God's economy.

Practical Steps to Experience This Reality

1. Daily Communion: Engage in regular prayer and fellowship with the Holy Spirit to maintain a vibrant connection with God.

2. Scripture Meditation: Reflect on the Word of God to renew your mind and align your thoughts with God's truth.

3. Obedience to the Spirit: Follow the promptings of the Holy Spirit, allowing Him to guide your actions and decisions.

4. Community Involvement: Participate actively in the life of the Church, fostering mutual growth and edification.

The Outcome of Dispensation

Living in accordance with God's economy results in a transformed life that reflects His glory. The ultimate goal is for the Triune God to be fully expressed through His Church, as Ephesians 3:19 states, "to know the love of Christ that surpasses knowledge, that you may be filled with all the fullness of God." This fullness is realized as we yield to God's work within us, allowing His life to permeate every aspect of our being.

Conclusion

Understanding and living by the principle of God's economy is essential for experiencing the fullness of His life. By recognizing the tripartite nature of man and the Church's role, we can align ourselves with God's divine plan. This alignment allows us to be vessels of His glory, manifesting His life and purpose in the world.

Islam:

1. Quranic Guidance:

- Moderation and Balance: The Quran advocates for moderation and balance in all aspects of life, including consumption. Surah Al-Isra (17:26-27) warns against extravagance, stating, "Indeed, the wasteful are brothers of the devils."

- Charity and Social Responsibility: Islam places a strong emphasis on zakat (obligatory almsgiving) and sadaqah (voluntary charity), promoting the redistribution of wealth and care for the needy (Surah Al-Baqarah 2:177).

2. Spiritual Fulfillment:

- Submission to Allah: Spiritual fulfillment in Islam comes from submission to Allah, adherence to His commandments, and striving for righteousness. The Five Pillars of Islam provide a framework for a balanced and meaningful life.

- Contentment and Gratitude: Islamic teachings encourage contentment (rida) and gratitude (shukr) for Allah's blessings, fostering an attitude of appreciation rather than constant desire for more.

Hinduism:

1. Philosophical Insights:

- Detachment and Simplicity: Hindu philosophy emphasizes detachment (vairagya) from material possessions and the pursuit of simplicity. The Bhagavad Gita (Chapter 2, Verse 47) advises, "You have a right to perform your prescribed duties, but you are not entitled to the fruits of your actions."

- Four Purusharthas: The concept of the four Purusharthas—Dharma (duty), Artha (wealth), Kama (pleasure), and Moksha (liberation)—provides a holistic approach to life, balancing material and spiritual pursuits.

2. Spiritual Fulfillment:

- Self-Realization: Hinduism teaches that true fulfillment comes from self-realization and union with the divine (Brahman). The practice of yoga and meditation helps individuals transcend material desires and achieve inner peace.

- Karma Yoga: The path of Karma Yoga emphasizes selfless action and service, encouraging individuals to perform their duties without attachment to outcomes.

Buddhism:

1. Teachings on Desire and Attachment:
- Four Noble Truths: The First Noble Truth acknowledges that suffering (dukkha) is an inherent part of life, and the Second Noble Truth identifies desire (tanha) and attachment as the primary causes of suffering.
- Eightfold Path: The Eightfold Path offers a way to overcome desire and attachment, promoting ethical conduct, mental discipline, and wisdom as means to achieve enlightenment.

2. Spiritual Fulfillment:
- Middle Way: Buddhism advocates for the Middle Way, a balanced approach to life that avoids extremes of self-

indulgence and self-mortification. This path leads to spiritual awakening and liberation from suffering.

   - Simplicity and Contentment: The practice of mindfulness and meditation fosters simplicity and contentment, helping individuals cultivate a sense of inner peace and fulfillment.

Judaism:

1. Ethical Teachings:
   - Tzedakah and Tikkun Olam: Jewish teachings emphasize tzedakah (charity) and tikkun olam (repairing the world) as central ethical imperatives. These concepts encourage the responsible use of wealth and the pursuit of social justice.

   - Sabbath and Festivals: The observance of the Sabbath and festivals provides a counterbalance to consumerism, emphasizing rest, spiritual reflection, and communal celebration over material pursuits.

2. Spiritual Fulfillment:
   - Covenantal Relationship: Spiritual fulfillment in Judaism comes from living in accordance with God's commandments and maintaining a covenantal relationship

with Him. This relationship prioritizes ethical behavior and spiritual growth over material accumulation.

- Study and Prayer: The study of Torah and regular prayer are essential practices that nurture spiritual fulfillment and a sense of connection to God and the community.

Conclusion

Consumerism, with its focus on material acquisition and external validation, often stands in stark contrast to the spiritual values emphasized in religious traditions. The pursuit of material wealth can lead to environmental degradation, social inequality, and personal dissatisfaction, while spiritual fulfillment is found in virtues such as simplicity, generosity, contentment, and ethical living. As we continue to explore the theology of money, it becomes clear that true fulfillment lies not in the accumulation of material goods but in the cultivation of a deeper, more meaningful connection to the divine and to our fellow human beings.

CHAPTER 18

STEWARDSHIP AND ENVIRONMENTAL ETHICS

The concept of stewardship is central to many religious traditions, emphasizing the responsible management of resources entrusted to humanity by a divine creator. This chapter explores theological perspectives on stewardship and environmental ethics, linking economic practices with the imperative to care for the Earth. We will examine how different faith traditions articulate the duty to protect the environment and promote sustainable economic practices.

Christian Perspectives on Stewardship

Christianity offers a rich tradition of teachings on stewardship, emphasizing the responsibility to care for creation as a divine mandate.

1. Biblical Foundations:

- Creation Mandate: The Bible presents humanity's role as stewards of God's creation. Genesis 1:28 describes God's command to "fill the earth and subdue it" and to "have dominion" over all living things. This dominion is interpreted as responsible stewardship rather than exploitation.

- Parable of the Talents: In Matthew 25:14-30, the Parable of the Talents emphasizes the importance of using resources wisely and faithfully. The servants are rewarded or punished based on how well they manage what they have been given.

2. Environmental Ethics:

- Laudato Si': Pope Francis' encyclical Laudato Si' (2015) calls for an integral ecology, linking care for the environment with social justice. The encyclical emphasizes that environmental degradation and social inequality are interconnected issues requiring a comprehensive response.

- Creation Care: Many Christian denominations advocate for "creation care," which involves adopting sustainable practices, reducing consumption, and protecting natural ecosystems as acts of worship and obedience to God.

Islamic Perspectives on Environmental Stewardship

Islamic teachings emphasize the concept of khalifah (stewardship) and the duty to protect and preserve the environment.

1. Quranic Guidance:

- Khalifah: The Quran describes humanity as Allah's khalifah (steward or vicegerent) on Earth, responsible for maintaining balance and harmony in creation (Surah Al-Baqarah 2:30). This role entails caring for the environment and using resources sustainably.

- Avoiding Corruption: The Quran warns against spreading corruption on Earth, which includes environmental harm (Surah Al-A'raf 7:31). Believers are encouraged to act justly and avoid wasteful practices (Surah Al-Isra 17:27).

2. Environmental Ethics:

- Ethical Consumption: Islamic teachings advocate for moderation and ethical consumption. The principle of halal (permissible) extends to ensuring that economic activities do not harm the environment.

- Green Mosques: Many Muslim communities are adopting sustainable practices, such as "green mosques" that incorporate renewable energy, water conservation, and waste reduction.

Hindu Perspectives on Environmental Stewardship

Hinduism offers a holistic view of the environment, emphasizing the interconnectedness of all life and the duty to protect nature.

1. Philosophical Foundations:

- Sacredness of Nature: Hindu texts and traditions regard nature as sacred and imbued with the divine. Rivers, mountains, and forests are often personified as deities, and their protection is seen as a religious duty.

- Ahimsa: The principle of ahimsa (non-violence) extends to all living beings and the environment. This ethic encourages minimizing harm to the natural world and promoting sustainability.

2. Environmental Ethics:

- Sustainable Living: Hindu teachings advocate for a lifestyle that balances material needs with spiritual values. Practices such as vegetarianism, organic farming, and water conservation are seen as expressions of environmental stewardship.

- Festivals and Rituals: Many Hindu festivals and rituals incorporate elements of environmental awareness, such as planting trees, cleaning rivers, and reducing waste.

Buddhist Perspectives on Environmental Stewardship

Buddhism emphasizes mindfulness, compassion, and the interdependence of all life, offering a profound basis for environmental ethics.

1. Philosophical Insights:

- Interconnectedness: The concept of pratitya-samutpada (dependent origination) highlights the interconnectedness of all life. This understanding fosters a sense of responsibility for the well-being of the environment.

- Middle Way: The Middle Way advocates for a balanced approach to life, avoiding extremes of consumption and asceticism. This principle supports sustainable and mindful living.

2. Environmental Ethics:

- Mindful Consumption: Buddhist teachings encourage mindful consumption, reducing desire and attachment to material goods. This practice helps minimize environmental impact and promotes sustainability.

- Engaged Buddhism: Engaged Buddhism integrates social and environmental activism with spiritual practice. Figures like Thich Nhat Hanh have emphasized the need for ecological mindfulness and active protection of the environment.

Jewish Perspectives on Environmental Stewardship

Judaism offers a framework for environmental stewardship rooted in the Torah and the ethical imperative to care for creation.

1. Biblical Teachings:

- Tikkun Olam: The concept of tikkun olam (repairing the world) reflects the Jewish commitment to social and environmental justice. It encompasses actions that improve and protect the natural world.

- Sabbath and Sabbatical Year: The observance of the Sabbath and the Sabbatical year (Shmita) promotes rest for the land and sustainable agricultural practices (Leviticus 25:1-7).

2. Environmental Ethics:

- Bal Tashchit: The principle of bal tashchit (do not destroy) prohibits wasteful destruction of resources. This ethic encourages conservation and sustainable use of the environment.

- Eco-Kashrut: The modern concept of eco-kashrut extends traditional dietary laws to include considerations of environmental impact, animal welfare, and sustainable farming.

Conclusion

Theological perspectives on stewardship and environmental ethics offer valuable insights into the responsible management of resources and the protection of the natural world. By linking economic practices with the ethical imperative to care for the environment, these teachings provide a framework for sustainable living that respects both human and ecological well-being. As we continue to explore the theology of money, the integration of environmental ethics with economic behavior underscores the importance of holistic stewardship in achieving a just and sustainable future.

CHAPTER 19

THE POSITIVE EFFECTS OF THE THEOLOGY OF MONEY IN OUR DAILY LIVES

The theology of money provides a framework for understanding and utilizing financial resources in ways that honor God and promote the well-being of individuals and communities. When approached from a theological perspective, money becomes a tool for good, fostering generosity, justice, and stewardship. This chapter explores the positive effects of the theology of money in our daily lives, highlighting how biblical principles can transform our financial practices and enrich our spiritual and communal experiences.

Cultivating Generosity

1. Biblical Mandate for Generosity:

- 2 Corinthians 9:6-7: "Remember this: Whoever sows sparingly will also reap sparingly, and whoever sows generously will also reap generously. Each of you should give what you have decided in your heart to give, not reluctantly or under compulsion, for God loves a cheerful giver."

- Commentary: The theology of money encourages believers to be generous, reflecting God's generosity towards us. Generosity fosters a spirit of gratitude and trust in God's provision, leading to a more fulfilling and joyful life.

2. Building Stronger Communities:

- Acts 2:44-45: "All the believers were together and had everything in common. They sold property and possessions to give to anyone who had need."

- Commentary: Generosity strengthens community bonds and ensures that everyone's needs are met. By sharing resources, believers create a supportive and caring environment that reflects the love of Christ.

Promoting Justice and Equity

1. Fairness in Economic Practices:

- Proverbs 11:1: "The Lord detests dishonest scales, but accurate weights find favor with him."

- Commentary: A theological approach to money emphasizes honesty and fairness in all financial dealings. Ethical business practices promote justice and equity, ensuring that economic systems benefit everyone fairly.

2. Advocating for the Poor:

- Isaiah 1:17: "Learn to do right; seek justice. Defend the oppressed. Take up the cause of the fatherless; plead the case of the widow."

- Commentary: The theology of money calls believers to advocate for social justice and support marginalized individuals. By using financial resources to address inequalities, Christians can help create a more just and compassionate society.

Encouraging Responsible Stewardship

1. Wise Management of Resources:

- Matthew 25:21: "His master replied, 'Well done, good and faithful servant! You have been faithful with a few things; I will put you in charge of many things. Come and share your master's happiness!'"

- Commentary: The parable of the talents teaches the importance of wise stewardship. Managing resources responsibly not only honors God but also leads to increased opportunities and blessings.

2. Sustainable Living:

- Genesis 2:15: "The Lord God took the man and put him in the Garden of Eden to work it and take care of it."

- Commentary: Responsible stewardship includes caring for the environment. Sustainable living practices that minimize waste and conserve resources reflect a commitment to God's creation and ensure the well-being of future generations.

Enhancing Personal Well-being

1. Freedom from Financial Anxiety:

- Matthew 6:31-33: "So do not worry, saying, 'What shall we eat?' or 'What shall we drink?' or 'What shall we wear?' For the pagans run after all these things, and your heavenly Father knows that you need them. But seek first his kingdom and his righteousness, and all these things will be given to you as well."

- Commentary: Trusting in God's provision alleviates financial anxiety and promotes a sense of peace. By prioritizing spiritual values over material concerns, believers can experience greater contentment and security.

2. Cultivating Contentment:

- Philippians 4:11-13: "I am not saying this because I am in need, for I have learned to be content whatever the circumstances. I know what it is to be in need, and I know what it is to have plenty. I have learned the secret of being content in any and every situation, whether well fed or hungry, whether living in plenty or in want. I can do all this through him who gives me strength."

- Commentary: The theology of money fosters contentment by encouraging a focus on God's sufficiency rather than material abundance. Contentment leads to a more balanced and satisfying life, free from the pressures of consumerism.

Strengthening Spiritual Growth

1. Aligning Finances with Faith:

- Matthew 6:21: "For where your treasure is, there your heart will be also."

- Commentary: The theology of money helps believers align their financial decisions with their faith. By investing in what matters to God, such as charity and community, believers can grow spiritually and deepen their relationship with Him.

2. Practicing Generosity as Worship:

- Hebrews 13:16: "And do not forget to do good and to share with others, for with such sacrifices God is pleased."

- Commentary: Generosity is an act of worship that pleases God. By giving to others, believers honor God and demonstrate His love, which fosters spiritual growth and a deeper sense of purpose.

Fostering Global Impact

1. Supporting Mission and Outreach:

- Acts 1:8: "But you will receive power when the Holy Spirit comes on you; and you will be my witnesses in Jerusalem, and in all Judea and Samaria, and to the ends of the earth."

- Commentary: Financial resources can be used to support mission and outreach efforts, spreading the gospel and meeting the needs of people worldwide. This global impact reflects the Great Commission and advances God's kingdom on earth.

2. Promoting Global Solidarity:

- Galatians 6:2: "Carry each other's burdens, and in this way, you will fulfill the law of Christ."

- Commentary: The theology of money encourages believers to support global initiatives that address poverty, injustice, and suffering. By carrying each other's burdens, Christians can promote global solidarity and reflect the unity of the body of Christ.

Conclusion

The theology of money offers a transformative approach to financial resources, emphasizing generosity, justice, stewardship, and spiritual growth. By aligning our financial practices with biblical principles, we can experience the positive effects of the theology of money in our daily lives. These effects include stronger communities, greater contentment, enhanced personal well-being, and a deeper relationship with God.

As believers, we are called to use our financial resources in ways that honor God and benefit others. By doing so, we participate in God's redemptive work in the world, reflecting His love and generosity. The positive effects of the theology of money are far-reaching, impacting our lives, our communities, and the world at large. Through faithful stewardship and generous giving, we can make a significant difference, advancing God's kingdom and promoting a just and compassionate society.

CHAPTER 20

THE NEGATIVE EFFECTS OF THE THEOLOGY OF MONEY IN OUR DAILY LIVES

While the theology of money can guide believers towards responsible and ethical financial practices, it can also be misinterpreted or misapplied, leading to negative consequences. When financial teachings are distorted or taken out of context, they can result in materialism, exploitation, and spiritual decline. This chapter explores the negative effects of the theology of money in our daily lives, highlighting the potential pitfalls and offering biblical insights to avoid these dangers.

Misinterpretation of Prosperity

1. Prosperity Gospel:

- 1 Timothy 6:9-10: "Those who want to get rich fall into temptation and a trap and into many foolish and harmful desires that plunge people into ruin and destruction. For the love of money is a root of all kinds of evil."

- Commentary: The prosperity gospel, which equates financial success with God's favor, can lead to materialism and spiritual corruption. This misinterpretation promotes the pursuit of wealth over spiritual growth, contrary to biblical teachings.

2. Materialism and Greed:

- Luke 12:15: "Then he said to them, 'Watch out! Be on your guard against all kinds of greed; life does not consist in an abundance of possessions.'"

- Commentary: A focus on material wealth can foster greed and a false sense of security. This mindset undermines the biblical call to seek first God's kingdom and leads to a shallow, possession-oriented life.

Exploitation and Inequality

1. Economic Exploitation:

- James 5:1-4: "Now listen, you rich people, weep and wail because of the misery that is coming on you. Your wealth has rotted, and moths have eaten your clothes. Your gold and silver are corroded. Their corrosion will testify against you and eat your flesh like fire. You have hoarded wealth in the last days. Look! The wages you failed to pay the workers who mowed your fields are crying out against you. The cries of the harvesters have reached the ears of the Lord Almighty."

- Commentary: Misapplication of financial teachings can lead to the exploitation of workers and unjust economic practices. This exploitation is condemned in Scripture and results in societal inequality and injustice.

2. Social Inequality:

- Proverbs 22:16: "Whoever oppresses the poor to increase his own wealth, or gives to the rich, will only come to poverty."

- Commentary: The misuse of money can exacerbate social inequalities, as wealth is concentrated among a few while many are left in poverty. This contradicts the biblical mandate for justice and care for the poor.

Spiritual Decline

1. Idolatry of Wealth:

- Matthew 6:24: "No one can serve two masters. Either you will hate the one and love the other, or you will be devoted to the one and despise the other. You cannot serve both God and money."

- Commentary: The idolatry of wealth can lead to spiritual decline, as individuals prioritize money over their relationship with God. This misplaced devotion detracts from true worship and spiritual growth.

2. Neglect of Spiritual Values:

- Revelation 3:17: "You say, 'I am rich; I have acquired wealth and do not need a thing.' But you do not realize that you are wretched, pitiful, poor, blind and naked."

- Commentary: Wealth can create a false sense of self-sufficiency and lead to the neglect of spiritual values. This spiritual complacency hinders one's relationship with God and stunts personal growth.

Disruption of Community and Relationships

1. Financial Conflicts:

- James 4:1-2: "What causes fights and quarrels among you? Don't they come from your desires that battle within you? You desire but do not have, so you kill. You covet but you cannot get what you want, so you quarrel and fight."

- Commentary: Money can be a source of conflict within communities and relationships. Financial disputes arise from covetousness and greed, disrupting harmony and fellowship.

2. Undermining Community Support:

- Acts 5:1-4: "Now a man named Ananias, together with his wife Sapphira, also sold a piece of property. With his wife's full knowledge, he kept back part of the money for himself but brought the rest and put it at the apostles' feet. Then Peter said, 'Ananias, how is it that Satan has so filled your heart that you have lied to the Holy Spirit and have kept for yourself some of the money you received for the land? Didn't it belong to you before it was sold? And after it was sold, wasn't the money at your disposal? What made you think of doing such a thing? You have not lied just to human beings but to God.'"

- Commentary: Dishonesty and deceit in financial matters can undermine trust within a community. Ananias and Sapphira's story illustrates the severe consequences of financial dishonesty, which disrupts communal support and integrity.

Misplaced Priorities

1. Neglect of the Poor:

- Matthew 25:45: "He will reply, 'Truly I tell you, whatever you did not do for one of the least of these, you did not do for me.'"

- Commentary: A theology of money that prioritizes personal wealth over helping the needy fails to align with Christ's teachings. Neglecting the poor and marginalized contradicts the call to serve and love others.

2. Temporal Focus Over Eternal Values:

- Colossians 3:2: "Set your minds on things above, not on earthly things."

- Commentary: An overemphasis on accumulating wealth shifts focus from eternal values to temporal concerns. This misalignment detracts from spiritual goals and fosters a materialistic mindset.

Addressing the Negative Effects

1. Biblical Accountability:

- Galatians 6:1-2: "Brothers and sisters, if someone is caught in a sin, you who live by the Spirit should restore that person gently. But watch yourselves, or you also may be tempted. Carry each other's burdens, and in this way you will fulfill the law of Christ."

- Commentary: The Christian community is called to hold each other accountable in financial practices. Gentle restoration and mutual support can help address and correct negative behaviors related to money.

2. Teaching and Discipleship:

- 2 Timothy 3:16-17: "All Scripture is God-breathed and is useful for teaching, rebuking, correcting and training in righteousness, so that the servant of God may be thoroughly equipped for every good work."

- Commentary: Teaching and discipleship rooted in Scripture are essential for correcting misinterpretations of the theology of money. Proper instruction helps believers align their financial practices with biblical principles, avoiding negative consequences.

Conclusion

While the theology of money offers valuable insights and guidance, its misinterpretation or misapplication can lead to significant negative effects. These include materialism, exploitation, spiritual decline, and disrupted relationships. By adhering to biblical teachings and maintaining accountability within the Christian community, believers can mitigate these negative effects and ensure that their financial practices honor God and promote justice, generosity, and stewardship.

Understanding and applying the theology of money correctly is crucial for fostering a healthy relationship with wealth and resources. By prioritizing eternal values, promoting justice, and practicing generosity, believers can navigate the challenges of financial stewardship and reflect the heart of God in their daily lives.

CHAPTER 21

THE FUTURE OF MONEY AND THEOLOGICAL REFLECTION

The future of money is shaped by rapid technological advancements, evolving economic systems, and changing societal values. This chapter speculates on the future of currency and the evolving theological considerations surrounding wealth. We will suggest ways faith communities can address emerging economic challenges, integrating theological principles with practical solutions.

The Evolution of Currency

1. Digital and Cryptocurrencies:
- Rise of Cryptocurrencies: Bitcoin, Ethereum, and other cryptocurrencies represent a significant shift in the

nature of money. These decentralized currencies challenge traditional banking systems and offer new ways of conducting transactions. As Proverbs 13:11 says, "Wealth gained hastily will dwindle, but whoever gathers little by little will increase it." The growth of cryptocurrencies highlights the importance of wisdom and patience in financial matters.

- Blockchain Technology: Blockchain technology, which underpins cryptocurrencies, promises greater transparency and security in financial transactions. This could lead to more ethical and accountable economic practices. Ephesians 4:28 encourages honest work and sharing, aligning with the transparency that blockchain can offer: "Let the thief no longer steal, but rather let him labor, doing honest work with his own hands, so that he may have something to share with anyone in need."

2. Central Bank Digital Currencies (CBDCs):

- Government Initiatives: Several central banks are exploring the development of digital currencies (CBDCs) to complement or replace physical cash. CBDCs could offer greater financial inclusion, efficiency, and control over monetary policy. Proverbs 22:7 reminds us of the influence of wealth: "The rich rules over the poor, and the borrower is the slave of the lender." Effective monetary policy through CBDCs could address such imbalances.

- Implications for Privacy and Control: While CBDCs can enhance efficiency, they also raise concerns about privacy and government surveillance. Balancing these issues will be crucial for their acceptance. The Bible warns in Proverbs 15:3, "The eyes of the Lord are in every place, keeping watch on the evil and the good," suggesting the importance of transparency and accountability.

3. Sustainable and Ethical Finance:

- Green Finance: The future of money increasingly incorporates environmental considerations, with investments in green technologies and sustainable practices gaining prominence. Ethical finance seeks to align economic activities with broader social and environmental goals. Genesis 2:15 underscores our responsibility to care for the Earth: "The Lord God took the man and put him in the garden of Eden to work it and keep it."

- Social Impact Investing: Investors are increasingly looking to support initiatives that generate positive social and environmental impacts alongside financial returns. This trend reflects a growing awareness of the interconnectedness of economic and ethical considerations. Proverbs 19:17 states,

"Whoever is generous to the poor lends to the Lord, and he will repay him for his deed."

Theological Reflections on Wealth and Currency

1. Ethical Use of Wealth:

- Redistribution and Charity: Religious teachings consistently emphasize the ethical use of wealth, advocating for redistribution and charitable giving. Faith communities can leverage digital platforms to enhance charitable efforts and ensure resources reach those in need. Luke 6:38 says, "Give, and it will be given to you. A good measure, pressed down, shaken together, and running over, will be poured into your lap. For with the measure you use, it will be measured to you."

- Fairness and Justice: Theological principles call for fairness and justice in economic practices. Faith communities can advocate for policies that reduce inequality and promote equitable wealth distribution. Micah 6:8 encourages us to "act justly and to love mercy and to walk humbly with your God."

2. Simplicity and Contentment:

- Countering Materialism: As consumerism and materialism continue to dominate, religious teachings on simplicity and contentment offer a counter-narrative. Faith communities can promote values that prioritize spiritual well-being over material accumulation. Philippians 4:11-12 teaches contentment: "I have learned in whatever situation I am to be content."

- Mindful Consumption: Encouraging mindful consumption and sustainable living aligns with theological principles and addresses the environmental impact of overconsumption. Ecclesiastes 5:10 warns, "He who loves money will not be satisfied with money, nor he who loves wealth with his income; this also is vanity."

3. Community and Mutual Support:

- Strengthening Community Bonds: Faith communities can foster stronger community bonds through cooperative economic practices, such as community savings groups, microfinance initiatives, and support networks. Acts 4:32 highlights the early Christian community's unity: "Now the full number of those who believed were of one heart and soul, and no one said that any of the things that belonged to him was his own, but they had everything in common."

- Economic Solidarity: The concept of economic solidarity, rooted in theological principles, encourages mutual support and collective action to address economic challenges.

Hebrews 13:16 reminds us, "Do not neglect to do good and to share what you have, for such sacrifices are pleasing to God."

Addressing Economic Challenges

1. Financial Inclusion:

- Access to Financial Services: Faith communities can advocate for greater financial inclusion, ensuring that marginalized and underserved populations have access to banking, credit, and investment opportunities. James 2:5 emphasizes God's concern for the poor: "Listen, my beloved brothers, has not God chosen those who are poor in the world to be rich in faith and heirs of the kingdom, which he has promised to those who love him?"

- Education and Empowerment: Providing financial literacy education and resources can empower individuals to make informed economic decisions and improve their financial well-being. Proverbs 16:16 values wisdom over wealth: "How much better to get wisdom than gold! To get understanding is to be chosen rather than silver."

2. Technological Adaptation:

- Embracing Innovation: Faith communities can embrace technological innovations, such as digital currencies and blockchain, to enhance transparency, efficiency, and security in financial transactions. Psalm 90:17 encourages God to establish the work of our hands: "Let the favor of the Lord our God be upon us, and establish the work of our hands upon us; yes, establish the work of our hands!"

- Ethical Guidelines: Developing ethical guidelines for the use of new technologies can help navigate the moral implications and ensure that technological advancements align with theological values. Proverbs 21:3 underscores the importance of righteousness and justice: "To do righteousness and justice is more acceptable to the Lord than sacrifice."

3. Advocacy and Policy:

- Influencing Policy: Faith communities can play a significant role in advocating for policies that promote economic justice, environmental sustainability, and social welfare. Engaging in public discourse and collaborating with policymakers can amplify their impact. Isaiah 1:17 calls us to "learn to do good; seek justice, correct oppression; bring justice to the fatherless, plead the widow's cause."

- Global Solidarity: Addressing global economic challenges requires a commitment to global solidarity. Faith communities can support international initiatives that tackle poverty, inequality, and environmental degradation. Galatians 6:2 encourages us to "bear one another's burdens, and so fulfill the law of Christ."

Conclusion

The future of money presents both opportunities and challenges that require careful theological reflection and practical action. By integrating ethical and theological principles with innovative economic practices, faith communities can address emerging challenges and promote a more just and sustainable economic future. As we conclude our exploration of the theology of money, it is clear that faith, ethics, and economics are deeply intertwined, and thoughtful engagement with these issues is essential for the well-being of both individuals and society.